Instagram Influencer Secrets

The Ultimate Strategy Guide to Passive Income, Social Media Marketing & Growing Your Personal Brand or Business

By Charlotte Sterling

Table of Contents

Don't have time to read?

Download the audiobook for FREE today on Audible. Then you can listen to this guide wherever you want, whenever you want.

US READERS

➡ **http://bit.ly/instagramsecretsus** ⬅

UK READERS

➡ **http://bit.ly/instagramsecretsuk** ⬅

Don't have time to read?

Download the audiobook for FREE today on Audible. Then you can listen to this guide wherever you want, whenever you want.

US READERS

➡ **http://bit.ly/instagramsecretsus** ⬅

UK READERS

➡ **http://bit.ly/instagramsecretsuk** ⬅

Preface

Thanks for downloading Instagram Influencer Secrets! #Yasqueen #lit🔥 #Influencerstatus.

Thought I'd throw in a few hashtags and emoji's for you to prepare you for what's to come. You're about to be thrown into a world where #hashtags will be your key to success, where writing comments and liking photos is the new way to make friends, and creating video content or live streams will bring you cash.

With this book, you are going to discover everything you need to know in order to understand and conquer Instagram so that you can expand your business into this incredible photo-sharing application. Instagram is not only a fascinating tool that you can leverage for your business, but it is also an incredibly fun experience that can be shared between both your brand and your customers. When used effectively, the empowering relationships that will be cultivated between you and your audience will both carry your company forward and fill your business with value and meaning.

Instagram is home to nearly 1 billion monthly active users who all come to Instagram to share, network, develop their businesses, and discover new companies to support and shop through. It is the second largest social networking site available, aside from Facebook which tops the charts with 1.4 billion active monthly users. Of those users, a massive 500 million daily users take to the site to browse their newsfeeds, connect with people and brands who interest them, and share their lives with their followers. Did you know that of these 500 million daily users, the "Like" button is hit at an average total of 4.2 billion times per day? That is an incredibly large number! As well, of those 500 million daily users, more than 200 million of them actively visit business profiles at least once per day. Getting found on Instagram is by far one of the easiest ways to massively grow your business without having to invest too much money into the marketing process.

Not only does Instagram have a higher number of users than almost any other social networking site out there, but it also has some of the best demographics in terms of *shoppers* hanging out on the network! In a recent study, it was discovered that Instagram's demographic is composed of a whopping 31% of users who make more than 75k per year. This means that almost one-third of the entire userbase has plenty of expendable money to spend on great products or services that they may stumble about during their daily scroll, such as yours! As long as you are doing your part in getting discovered, Instagram is a great opportunity to connect with potential customers, build relationships with your target audience, and maximize your brand exposure.

A common worry when it comes to building a business online is that the amount of competition may be too large to really make the effort worth it. This is a natural concern when you see such large numbers and realize that Instagram marketing has grown to become such a hot topic in the business world. However, as of early 2018, only 28% of all Instagram users were actually using the platform to market their businesses, the other 72% were only using it for personal purposes. Furthermore, of that 28% of the active user population, many of those businesses will still be comprised of individuals who may be a part of your target audience! Just because they are running their own businesses does not mean that they are not actively ready to purchase things that interest them, especially if you are taking advantage of the platform correctly.

One of the reasons why Instagram is so valuable to marketers is because the platform sees about 4% of their total followers engaging their posts on a regular basis. This is 10 times more engagement than most brands see on Facebook, which means that focusing your effort on Instagram is definitely the way to go if you are looking for a maximum return on your time investment. As well, according to a recent study, more than 70% of users will look up brands on Instagram to get a better idea of the brands "feeling" and to see what else they offer. If you are not on Instagram, you are missing out on a massive opportunity to connect with anyone who may come across your brand and then struggle to find you in the online space.

If you still are unsure as to whether or not Instagram is the right tool for you, just consider the following brands who have significantly grown their businesses using Instagram. Nike, a fitness brand, boasts 73.3 million followers and is one of the leading fitness brands on the entire network. The pictures Nike posts set the bar for social brand identity when it comes to the fitness industry as everything they share heavily embraces the fitness lifestyle rather than solely focusing on their products. As a result, they have managed to massively increase their following and held the #1 position for fitness brands until they recently slipped into second place as Nat Geo took the lead. ASOS, another massive company on Instagram, has built an entire legacy on Instagram surrounding the promotion of sub-accounts that work as brand ambassadors. ASOS is a fashion company that seeks to inspire confidence and empowerment in all of their 7.7 million followers on Instagram. Another massive brand that has taken Instagram by storm is Starbucks, who shares their posts with 14.9 million followers and used the platform to completely reinvent itself. Starbucks once held the ranking as being the most popular brand on Instagram and is known to leverage the power of user-generated content by encouraging people to photograph their fancy beverages and snacks and share them on the popular social sharing site.

Instagram is perhaps one of the best marketing tools for businesses to rely on because it thrives on picture sharing. They say that a picture says a thousand words, and when it comes to marketing your business you can use all one thousand of those words to say everything that you need to say about your brand. From portraying the tone of your brand to the image it has and the way it makes people feel, you can capture a lot in a single graphic, especially if it is done right. By taking the right graphics and marketing them properly on Instagram, you can have a massive impact on growing your brand through this one simple social networking tool. In addition, if you do not feel like expending a large budget to really get your name out there, Instagram does not require you to invest anything to get started since it is a free social networking site. While there are paid promotional options, they are not necessary since there are plenty of organic options that you can take advantage of as well.

If you are ready to begin discovering just how this social network can help you leverage your brand, earn a massive number of loyal followers, and convert those followers into paying customers, let us begin!

1 Understanding Your Goals and Motivation

Before you ever begin doing anything for your business, it is always important that you take the time to outline your goals and determine whether or not your ideal strategy is going to help you reach those goals. In the case of Instagram, simply knowing that there are a plethora of users out there ready to learn about companies like yours is not enough. Naturally, I think Instagram is an excellent tool for anyone to take advantage of. However, it is important that you go beyond basic statistics and really dig into *how* Instagram is going to be of value of you. This way, you know what you can expect going into the process of building your account and you can use your goals to help you determine your strategic action.

In this chapter, we are going to identify what your Instagram goals should be and how you can use Instagram to actually help you achieve those goals. It is important that you complete this step, even if you already have a general idea of what it is that you want to achieve. Let me guess, it was along the lines of *"I want a larger audience"* and *"I want more profit"*? These are two great goals, but unless you truly understand *exactly* how Instagram can benefit you in reaching these goals, or any other goals you may have, you will not achieve the results you want. They say in business you should never take an uncalculated risk and that time is money. Consider this step your process of calculating the risk so that your time investment is worth the exchange.

Why Are You On Instagram?

First, let us get your initial goal out of the way. The very goal or interest that led you to purchase this book and start learning about how you can leverage Instagram is likely going to be your primary goal when it comes to building your Instagram account. I want you to open up a document on your computer or grab your notebook and write this goal down at the top of your page. Be really clear about what it is, and make sure it is one that will help you increase the success of your business. What is it that you truly want? An increased audience base? Are you trying to sell more products? Do you want to access customers across the globe? Are you interested in driving more traffic to your website? Be clear in what you are seeking to achieve with your Instagram marketing strategies so that you know exactly what you are trying to achieve. This goal is going to be your primary objective when it comes to building your account, deciding what strategies to use, and measuring whether or not you are generating success through the strategies you have tried.

Underneath your main goal, I want you to jot down two or three reasons why you chose Instagram specifically and what you think Instagram has to offer that your other methods of marketing do not currently provide. We will go further into detail on these later, but doing this now will help you keep yourself focused and researching in the right direction. Consider this your framework to your overall goal setting and strategizing when it comes to your Instagram account.

Lastly, I want you to jot down how you think Instagram is going to tie in with your other marketing efforts and where you see it fitting into your overall marketing strategy. In doing so, you will begin to encourage yourself to see how Instagram will fit in as one piece of your larger puzzle and what your true purpose is when it comes to using Instagram for your brand. This is going to help you keep everything in perspective so that as you go on to strategize your Instagram efforts you can ensure that they are working effectively alongside all of your other marketing efforts too. If you are using Instagram exclusively at this time, consider what other avenues you plan on reaching out into as well and write them down for now. Even if you are not building into these avenues yet, having a good idea of where they will fit into will help you develop your Instagram presence in a way that eventually supports your successful efforts elsewhere.

Brainstorming Your Goals

Now that you know what your primary objective is on Instagram, it is time for you to start brainstorming the goals that you have for your efforts. Think about the tools that Instagram can offer for your business or personal brand; will they help you achieve your goal? For example, perhaps your goal is to "Increase your sales by 20% annually". You could leverage Instagram stories to run advertisements to drive customers to your website and purchase your products.

With that in mind, let's get clear on what *else* you want to achieve on Instagram, aside from your primary objective. Are you trying to improve your sales numbers? Develop more brand awareness? Target more influencers who can get your brand and products out there in a more influential manner? Be really clear on everything you want to achieve with your account so that you have a series of goals that you can be working towards, in addition to fulfilling your primary objective. This will help you build your Instagram account in a more dynamic manner so that you are not pushing too hard to achieve one specific goal. You want your Instagram to be a well-rounded tool, not a catalogue where you shove one style of content in everyone's faces and hope it pays off.

As you do the research for the following three sections, consider jotting down some potential goals you might set for yourself on Instagram. You should be jotting down a range of goals from short-term to long-term, with many different focuses on how they will serve you and benefit your business. This way when it comes to setting your official goals you can recall exactly what Instagram can help you with and then determine which of those goals mean the most to you. While you can always pursue all of them, it is a better idea to pursue the most meaningful or important ones first and then begin pursuing the less important ones later once you have begun seeing success in your prioritized goals. By building your goals in this manner, you will already have the framework for your Instagram strategies going forward.

How Will Instagram Help Your Brand?

The first thing that you need to consider when it comes to developing your Instagram goals is to identify how Instagram can help your unique brand. Each brand has something different to offer, so every company will have different benefits when it comes to leveraging Instagram for their marketing efforts. For some, Instagram may be a tool used to help them convey parts of the business that are rarely seen by the public, thus allowing them to paint a fuller picture for their audience. For example, a dentist office may use Instagram to speak more about general hygiene, new dental techniques, or the general passion that their dentists have for their patients. In doing so, the dentist office goes from being a potentially scary destination that people may avoid to becoming a trustworthy place where people feel safe in the hands of knowledgeable and compassionate staff.

For other businesses, Instagram may be used as a tool to give their brand an *actual identity*. These days, many businesses run their companies exclusively in the online space, abandoning all expenses of having a traditional brick-and-mortar business with physical marketing materials and other costly expenses. As a result, building into social media platforms like Instagram offers them a unique opportunity to actually give their brand a face and build an approachable personality for their customers to interact with.

This leads to the development of a term called *Influencers*. These are individuals, who have created a brand for themselves, otherwise known as a *personal brand* and have amassed such a large following that they are *influencing* their follower's decisions. They have a large fan-base, who follow the fashion trends, recommendations, etc of this individual and hang onto every word the Influencer says. When someone reaches an "Influencer" status, they will likely be approached by brands to do sponsorships or might even be paid hundreds of dollars per post just to be seen using their products. Many individuals are making passive income, or using their Influencer status as essentially a career. An example is Tara Milk Tea *@taramilktea* , who started her account as a food blogger. Now she gets invited to travel the world and take extravagant photos at the most breathtaking places. Her unique photography style and color themes make her stand out above the crowd.

How Instagram is going to support you ultimately depends on how you see it fitting in with your brand strategy. The best way to get an idea of what Instagram can help you with is to determine what type of business you own, what your primary objective is, and how Instagram may be supportive in helping you meet that objective. You can also browse around at other similar profiles to get an idea of how other similar companies are using Instagram for their own businesses. This way, you can get a visual idea of how Instagram is working for them, which strategies are used best, and which objectives are most likely to be met using the Instagram platform.

How Much Are You Willing To Invest?

Anytime you look towards developing a new business strategy, you should always consider what you are honestly willing to invest into said strategy and whether or not it will be enough based on the minimum requirements of the strategy itself. Fortunately, Instagram is a platform that can be modified to meet many different requirements. You can use it as much or as little as you want, to a degree, and for the most part, as long as you are using it correctly you should still be able to get consistently positive results out of your efforts.

Instagram is a platform that requires a time investment, and that can also benefit from having a budgeted investment involved, too. In terms of time investment, you need to consider how many minutes per day, or per week, you are willing to invest in building your profile. This is going to ensure that you are willing to invest enough time that it will be worth it. It will also help you decide what types of goals you can reasonably set with your time investment. From a financial perspective, you do not necessarily need a monetary budget to invest in your Instagram marketing, but it is valuable as it can accelerate your ability to be discovered and connect with potential customers. If you plan to set a budget aside for your Instagram marketing efforts, think about how much you would be willing to invest and how this might impact your goals.

How Is Instagram The Better Choice?

Lastly, you need to consider if Instagram will be more effective in accomplishing your objective, as compared to the other social platforms or marketing strategies out there. This does not mean that you cannot span your objective across multiple platforms; most brands will do this. However, it does mean that you need to decide whether or not Instagram is the right investment of your time and money *right now*.

If you feel that Instagram does have everything you need in order to expand effectively, then chances are Instagram is a great choice for you. Again, I genuinely believe that every brand needs to be on Instagram and building their platform as soon as possible since Instagram offers so many valuable resources and benefits. However, if for some reason you do not feel that your own objectives will be met through Instagram, you might consider slightly adjusting your objectives to fit the platform's abilities. This way, you can still gain the benefits of being on Instagram in a way that meets your needs and the investment that you are willing to make into the platform itself.

* * *

Action Step: Setting Your Goal

Now that you have done your research into Instagram and discovered everything that it has to offer, and how those benefits can support your business, it is time to start setting your goals for Instagram! This part is really easy, especially if you have actively been writing down all of the aforementioned tips and points I suggested along the way.

Step 1: Understand your objective

The first thing you are going to want to do is to consider your overall objective and what large goals are going to help you meet that objective. Generally your objective is quite broad. It answers a *What* rather than a *How*. I want you to be specific here, using numbers so your success can be quantified later on. Some examples might be:

- *Increase my revenue by $1,000 a month*
- *Improve customer satisfaction by 4%*
- *Attract more monthly visitors to my website, to 2,000 a month.*

Step 2: Break your objective into long term goals

Now you need to answer *how will you achieve this objective?* Your long term goals will help you answer this question. This will help you stay on track and see if you are working in the right direction to accomplish your objective. You should set at least 2-3 long-term goals that you are working towards when it comes to developing your purpose for Instagram. These goals do not all need to be achieved at the same time, either. You can easily set goals for six, twelve, and eighteen-month timeframes if that feels like the best course of action for you. Or, you can set out to have a few different goals that you want to have achieved within one year of being on your Instagram account. You can set these goals in whatever way works best for you.

It is important that your long-term goals directly reflect what your primary objective is with Instagram. Let's say your objective is to develop a strong sales funnel and you want to use Instagram as a part of that funnel to help get customers over to your website and purchasing your products. Your long term goals might look like:

- *Have 10,000 followers in one year*
- *See at least 4% engagement rates on my posts*
- *Have at least a 3% click-through rate on my website link*

These types of goals directly reflect your overall intention of driving people to your website through Instagram, meaning that they are constructive to your primary objective.

Step 3: Set milestones or short term goals

The next goals you want to set are your short-term goals. These goals are going to be set, met, and reset on a regular basis so it is important that you think in terms of making these goals both manageable and achievable when setting them. Because you are going to be moving through these smaller goals so rapidly, it is okay if you set the goal a bit too low or too high early on as you begin to get an understanding of what it is that you can reasonably achieve with your profile. As you go forward, you can begin setting these goals more realistically and achieving them with greater ease, using them as a tool to move you towards the successful completion of your long-term goals and primary objective.

The best way to go about setting your short-term goals is to set milestones for what you want these goals to achieve along the way. Then, you can create a set of mini-goals on a weekly or monthly basis to help keep you on track for achieving these goals going forward. For example, say your long-term goal is to have 10,000 followers at the 1 year mark, you may set the smaller goals of growing by at least 2,500 followers per quarter. Your mini-goals, then, would be based on helping you achieve that growth, such as by testing out new posting strategies or hashtags to see how you can maximize your growth and move towards your goal intentionally and effectively.

2 Identifying Your Audience

Now that you have an understanding of what you want to achieve with Instagram, it is time to start building your marketing strategy for your brand in Instagram-Land. The first step in building a strong strategy is knowing exactly who your audience is, as they are going to be the foundation upon which your entire strategy lies. While the general structure of the strategy remains the same, how you communicate with your audience will vary depending on your demographic. Each unique demographic speaks in a different way, relates to different experiences, and uses Instagram for different purposes, meaning that you are going to have to position yourself in a way that caters to your target audience.

In this chapter, you are going to discover why your target audience matters, how you can identify who they are, and what you need to do in order to design a brand that caters directly to your target audience. This will include important information on your language, tone, image, and keywords and hashtags that you will use when it comes to getting in touch with your audience. By putting these pieces of the puzzle together you can develop a solid strategy that helps get you directly in front of the people who are most likely to do business with you.

Why Your Target Audience Matters

There is a saying in the marketing world that goes "if you try talking to everyone, you will end up talking to no one." This speaks to the fact that if you attempt to make your brand liked by everyone, you will have a weak structure and it will be unclear as to who would benefit most from your products or services. For that reason, you need to narrow in on who you plan on marketing to and be really clear with defining your target audience. You want to get to know your target audience so well that you can easily become friends with them through your marketing efforts.

Because you need your audience to be narrow and specific, it is imperative that you are marketing to the person who is most likely to buy your products. Even though the range of people who are likely to be interested in learning more is probably quite large, the demographic of people who will actually pay for your products will be smaller. Add these people to your target audience. That way, you are marketing directly to the people who are most likely to be converted into clients and earn you a profit in your business.

Identifying Who Your Audience Is

Identifying who your target audience is starts with you doing some market research to discover which demographics exist in your industry. The best way to do this is to run a basic Google search on your industry using a phrase like, "[Industry] demographics [current year]." This way, you get relevant and updated information on who the demographics in your target audience actually are. Once you have an idea of the general audience, you need to start narrowing in on who is most likely to actually pay for what you are selling. You can do this by looking at your direct competitors and getting an idea of who they are advertising to and who is purchasing their products.

In order to use your competitors for this type of market research, you want to start by looking for your direct competitors and then looking at their Instagram page. Choose competitors who are well ahead of you in their businesses and who have already established a matured audience, or an audience whom they have maintained for a longer period of time. You can also look to see where else they are spending time online to get a better idea of who their overall audience is since most platforms tend to cater to different demographics in general. After finding your direct competitors, you can begin looking into who follows them, who engages their content the most, and who is actually buying their products. If they are on Instagram, look to see if they have a special hashtag that they encourage their customers to use. If they do, you can search that hashtag and get a sense of who is buying their products and loving them enough to actually tag them when they wear them. This will give you a stronger idea of who their active target audience is.

The last part of your competition that you need to pay attention to is their language and their marketing materials. Based on what they are posting, the language they are using, and the hashtags they are tagging, who does it sound like they are talking to? This can give you a good idea as to exactly who they have identified as their target audience and who you need to be targeting as well as how.

Understanding Your Instagram-Specific Demographics

Not all of your targeted demographic is going to be on Instagram. Despite having an incredibly large number of active users per month, Instagram is not the only location that your audience is going to be hanging around on. This is why it is important that you look at your competitors as a whole and see who they are targeting, and how, across various platforms. This will help you get a better idea of who your whole audience is, and which part of that audience you need to be targeting on Instagram.

The methods you use on Instagram should not be identical to the ones you use elsewhere online, or offline. Although you want to keep your branding, personality, and purpose the same across all platforms, you also want to make sure that you are speaking in a way that caters to that specific part of your audience that is unique to each platform. A great way to get a better understanding of your Instagram-specific demographic is to take a look at your general target audience, especially if you already have an established audience, and then look at Instagram's demographics overall. You can easily find updated information on Instagram's unique demographics through a quick Google search. Then, you can compare their demographics versus your own to get an idea of which part of your audience you should be paying attention to most in the Instagram space. That way, you are always talking to the right people and your marketing efforts are always paying off.

Locating Your Target Demographic On Instagram

Now that you know who you are talking to, you need to find them! On Instagram, the best way to begin locating your target audience is to search for them based on hashtags that are relevant to your industry, or through your competitor's accounts. Through both of these methods, you are going to discover where they spend their time based on what they are likely to search up, who they are following, and how they are interacting through their profile.

When it comes to hashtags, the easiest way to identify where your audience is would be to begin discovering hashtags that are relevant to your niche and then searching these hashtags on Instagram. You will learn more about discovering the best hashtags below. By looking up niche-specific hashtags on Instagram, you can start following accounts that are owned by people who would be considered a part of your target audience. You can also begin looking at *their* pictures and identifying what hashtags they are likely to be using, and then follow hashtags that are popular for your demographic, even if they are not specific to your industry. That way, you can hang out with your demographic online and gain access to them in as many ways as you can.

Another incredible way to discover your demographic is to look up hashtags that are relevant to your industry and then take a peek at what "similar" hashtags exist according to Instagram. This is a great way to locate more areas that your audience is hanging out on, allowing you to gain the opportunity to spend more time with them in many areas rather than just one. For example, if you look up *#yoga*, your suggested similar hashtags may include: *#yogi, #yogateacher, #selfpractice, #mindfulness, #meditation, #baliretreat* or any other number of hashtags. Make sure that you are using as many as you can, while staying relevant to your post, so that you can maximize your visibility on Instagram.

Finding demographics through your competitors is valuable because these are exactly the audience you want to be targeting, so there is no guessing. By going back to the same competitors that you looked up previously, you can start scrolling through their post "likes" and discovering who seems to be the most common when it comes to interacting with their content. If they have many comments on their posts, look these up as well as people who go the extra mile to comment are more likely to be a hot lead instead of a general lead.

Keyword and Hashtag Research

Keywords and hashtags are going to be your primary opportunity to connect with your target audience when it comes to Instagram. Through using keywords and hashtags effectively, you will be able to both identify where your target audience hangs out and "show up at the party" so to speak. This is how you are going to discover your audience, and how they are going to discover you. The keywords that you use on Instagram are not going to be the same as the ones you use elsewhere, so if you have already identified keywords for other areas in your business you are going to need to start again for your Instagram account.

On Instagram, keywords are not nearly as important as hashtags are since Instagram actually lacks a dedicated keyword research function. Instead, you want to pay attention to hashtags, which are Instagram's alternatives to keywords. Hashtags are the tags that people post at the end of their captions that look like this: #sample and they are used to help people discover feeds filled with images surrounding topics they are interested in. A fitness enthusiast, for example, could type in #fitness on Instagram and they would be shown millions of photos relating to fitness.

When it comes to getting identified on Instagram, you want to identify hashtags that are relevant to your brand but that are not quite so obvious. More broad hashtags have been used for so long and are used so frequently that they are not the best option if you are looking to get found. For example, a busy hashtag that gets 10 new tags per minute is going to result in you getting shoved out of the recent feed really quickly whereas one that only gets 10 new tags per hour is going to keep you around longer. Plus, if you can make it to the "Top Posts" spot on a less used (but still popular) hashtag, you are more likely to keep it for a longer period of time, making you easier for people to discover.

Although hashtags really are the primary opportunity to get found on Instagram, keywords do matter to an extent. On Instagram, posts with popular keywords are more likely to be shown in native newsfeeds over any other posts as Instagram deems them as relevant. While this will not impact where you show up on the "Recent post" feeds under hashtags, it will decide whether or not you show up in the newsfeed of your users. The best way to research keywords for your Instagram account is to use a third-party app like WordStream which will give you access to a full list of keywords that are relevant to your niche on Instagram specifically.

* * *

Action Step: Building Your Customer Profile

Now that you know who you are targeting, it is time for you to put all of that information together and develop your **target persona**. Your target persona is essentially the generic "profile" for who your target audience would be. The best way to look at it is that you are building the profile of your perfect client, complete with exactly who they are, what interests them, and why they are excited to do business with your brand. Some people will even go so far as to give their target persona a pretend name and build them as though they are a real person. For some individuals, turning their target persona into a character is a great way to see their audience as real and develop a dialogue with them that is personable and open.

In case you are not interested in completely building an avatar of your ideal client in that much significant detail, there is absolutely no need for you to worry! Your target persona does not have to be quite so detailed in order to be effective. As long as you are extremely clear about who you are talking to, this should be more than plenty to help you target your target audience and move forward effectively.

The following pieces of information are things you should be including in your target persona profile:

- Career (your target personas career tells you about what they are passionate about and what they encounter in life. For example, a lawyer is likely passionate about justice and experiences high stress.)
- Job Title
- Key information about their company
- Details about their role
- Demographics (your target personas demographic tells you what values they have, what they believe, how they speak, and what is important to them. It will also tell you what they can afford and if they will be willing to spend the extra expense on your products or services.)
- Age
- Gender
- Salary
- Location (urban/suburban/rural)
- Education
- Family
- Goals and Challenges (your target personas goals and challenges tells you what they are working towards in life, what they are passionate about, and what their pain points are.)
- Primary goal
- Secondary goal
- How you can help them
- Primary challenge
- Secondary challenge
- How you can help them

- Values and fears (your target personas values and fears tell you what they are going to prioritize above anyone else, and why they may object or have fears towards doing business with you)
- Primary values
- Common objections during the sales process

If you can successfully fill out this customer profile based on the information that you have discovered throughout this chapter, then you must know that you have a clear enough understanding of your target audience to be able to effectively connect with them. Make sure that you never guess when it comes to looking up the information to fulfil each of these questions. Instead, go find your target audience on Instagram and look over several profiles so that you can identify the trends and discover *exactly* who you are selling to. That way, you are not wasting your time attempting to market to an audience that does not actually exist. Even having minor errors in your target persona can result in you missing the mark completely, so be very precise in this practice so that you don't waste time trying to target the wrong people.

3 Designing Your Account

Now that you know your objective and who you are targeting, you need to design your Instagram account so that you can start interacting with people and getting your brand out there. Building your Instagram profile properly is essential: your profile is the foundation upon which everything else will be built. If you do not have it designed properly, it will not back your brand up with the clear, distinct, and powerful presentation that you need in order to truly succeed.

In this chapter, we are going to discover how you can develop a basic account for your business, what you need to consider, and how you can personalize it effectively. It is important that you follow each step carefully and that you leave nothing up to chance, not even the name of your profile or the design you use. If you do, you may end up designing an account that is not actually appealing to your target audience, resulting in all your research going to waste. If your profile looks exactly like the kind your target audience will be looking for, then it will be far more likely to encourage them to follow you and remember you than it does if it looks completely different from their interests.

The Basics Of Creating An Instagram Account

If you do not already have an Instagram account, you are going to need to start one. The easiest way to do this is to download the app onto your phone and then follow the prompts to sign up. You will need to use your email or phone number, develop a username and password, and give Instagram some basic information about you to get started. Before you get started, read "Choosing Your Instagram Handle" below so that you choose a username that is going to be great for business. If you already have an account, you can easily adjust your name if you need to by going into your profile settings and changing your username.

Instagram offers two different types of accounts: personal accounts and business accounts. Personal accounts offer all of the basic features of Instagram and, according to some people, are also easier to gain followers on. Business accounts offer more features such as analytics tracking, paid promotions, a call to action button on your profile, a location, and some other unique features. However, some people claim that when using a business account on Instagram it can be a little harder to grow your following organically due to the way the Instagram algorithm works.

Which type of account you choose to build will ultimately depend on what you are looking for from your Instagram account. If you want to be able to do in-app tracking, host paid promotions, and add a call to action to your profile you will want to turn "on" the business features for your account. You can do this in the settings menu. All of the information you need to know about customizing your business profile will be shared in Chapter 4. In the meantime, let us take a look at what else you need to know when building your Instagram account.

Setting Yourself Up For Success From Day 1

It is imperative that you set your Instagram account up for success starting on day 1. If you have already created an account, now is the perfect time to start paying attention to how you can modify your account to perfect it for building your business. Depending on how old your account is, you may want to erase all of your posts and start fresh so that your new followers do not get confused or thrown off by your old content.

As you go into creating your account, you want to think about what your clients are going to be thinking about when they land on your page. Ultimately, the best way to consider this is to look at the 5W + H. Your followers are going to first want to know who you are, what you are selling, when you are posting (paying attention to if you are relevant or updated regularly,) where you are located, why you matter, and how they can do business with you. If you can answer all of these questions on your profile, then it becomes infinitely easier for your audience to land on you, quickly identify you as meaningful and valuable, and then choose to follow you and hopefully check out your website, too.

The way that you are going to answer these questions for your audience is simple. You will do so by having an effective profile that has the right username, bio, profile photo, and feed to answer all of these questions in a quick glance. You may also choose to take advantage of story highlights to answer this for you, which essentially consists of you choosing your favorite stories and grouping them together under highlight reels on your profile. By landing on your profile and quickly glancing at all of these pieces your audience can determine right away whether or not you are a profile that looks interesting to them, or if they are disinterested and want to move on. If you have followed the next steps correctly and designed your profile properly, your audience will preferably choose to stick around and check out your content.

Choosing Your Instagram Handle

Your Instagram handle needs to be clear, simple, and easy to identify. You want to avoid using numbers or special characters in your profile handle because this will result in you being too challenging to find. The best handle you should use is just your business name, just like Nike (@nike), Walmart (@walmart), YumBakery (@yumbakery), TasteMade (@tastemade), NoRootsBoots (@norootsboots), and Target (@target) have. Using your business name is simple, easy to identify, and really starts building up brand awareness around your business so that people are more likely to recognize you in the future.

If your brand name is your name, you can simply use your name. However, this may not be ideal if your name is long, difficult to spell, or used by someone else already. In this case, you may want to shorten it to your first and middle name only or nickname like Jenni Farley of Jersey Shore did (@jwoww). Alternatively, if it is relevant to your business you may be able to add a simple prefix or suffix like Amanda Frances, a popular self-help personality, has done with her account (@xoamandafrances). Other examples of self-titled Instagram accounts that perform well and support in growing brand recognition include the ones held by Kim Kardashian

(@kimkardashian), Oprah (@oprah), Deepak Chopra (@deepakchopra), Jess C Lively (@jessclively), or Will Smith (@willsmith).

The only time in which a special character may be deemed acceptable is if you use a period, which some companies have used. However, this can become very confusing for your followers as they may find themselves going to the original profile that has no special characters, rather than finding yours. For that reason, you should completely avoid adding special characters, strange spelling, or other unique elements to your handle. The more simple it is, the better it will be as it will make it much easier for your followers to find you online.

Writing A Bio That Sells

On Instagram, you are offered a 150 character bio where you can give people an idea of who you are, what you stand for, and why they should be interested in your business. This bio is short, so you need to use your character count wisely so that you can say everything you need to say. You also need to make sure that you are keeping your bio catchy and interesting so that people are attracted to it and curious to learn more about when they find your profile.

When it comes to writing a bio that sells, there are a few different things you can consider that will help you really sell your profile and encourage people to follow you and check in frequently. The first thing you can try is isting your skills on your profile. This is especially helpful if you work alone, such as if you are an influencer, personal trainer, or fashion model. Saying something like "Recipes | Fitness Tips | Holistic Living | Plant-Powered" is a great way to show what you are all about and make it simple for your followers to know exactly who you are and what you offer.

If you want to use more complete sentences, you can use a motto or a quote that is relevant to your audience. For example, Milk Makeup's bio says "It's not just about how you create your look; it's what you do in it that matters. #liveyourlook" This type of bio shows your potential customers what matters to you, and quickly helps them determine whether your values are aligned or not.

Adding your email to your Instagram bio is always a good idea too, particularly if you are using a personal profile or if your business call to action is not based on emailing you. You can provide your email as a way for people to contact you, making it easy for potential customers, collaborators, or the press to get in touch with you to learn more.

If you have a tagline that you use in your brand, you might consider adding that to your profile, too. For example, Nike's tagline is "Just Do It" and their Instagram bio says: "If you have a body, you are an athlete. #justdoit" Adding your motto to your bio is a great way to start making your motto recognizable while also sharing what matters to you and your brand on Instagram.

Using emoticons in your bio is a good idea as long as these emoticons are relevant to what you are saying and what your overall brand image is. You should use emoticons sparingly to avoid overwhelming your potential followers or looking tacky to them. Emoticons can be a great way to build your image, space out your bio a bit to make it easier to read and convey the tone of voice that you are communicating with.

Make sure that your bio is relevant to your brand and your customer. You do not want to be using a funny bio if your audience is more likely to respond to an inspiring one any more than you want to be using a meaningful one if your audience is more likely to respond to a funny one. Use the proper language and tone to communicate with your audience effectively so that they instantly relate and are more likely to follow you.

Lastly, if you have a link to your website or somewhere else that you would like to guide your followers to you can place that link in the same area as where your bio goes. Placing a link on your account will help build Instagram into your funnel so that you can begin converting followers to customers!

Choosing Your Profile Picture

On Instagram, you have a small profile picture that is featured directly on your profile. This picture cannot be clicked or blown up, so it is important that you choose a profile picture that does not feature too many different details or too much texture as this can make your profile picture look confusing, distracting, or thoughtless. You want to use one that is clear, simple, and distinct. If you are building a brand, a great option for this image is your brand logo. Using your brand logo in this space will start building up recognition around what your brand looks like and how people can identify you in the online space.

If you are building your brand around your personal identity, such as if you are a brand influencer or a realtor, using a high-quality image of your own face for the profile picture is a great option too. It is important that the image you choose does not look too casual or busy, however, as this will make it distracting and confusing. Instead, choose an image that makes sense to your brand and that has a clear focus and plain background. If you are a fitness influencer, for example, having a portrait of you in a gym or working out would be a great image for you to use on your profile picture. Make sure that the gym is dimmed out and that you are clearly the highlight of the image and easy to see. If you are in a more professional position, such as if you are a doctor or a lawyer, having a plain background is preferred as this portrays a professional image that will help communicate your brand more effectively.

It is important that you avoid using stock images, product images, or images of objects in your profile picture as this can be confusing and may prevent people from clicking through to your profile. There is an exception to this rule, however. If you are a photographer, for example, a great photograph you have taken can be used in place of your profile image if your username and/or name on your profile clearly explain that you are a photographer. Another instance where this rule may be bent is if you are running a news program: some daily news sites will post a picture of their city's iconic skyline to add more depth and definition into their profile. If you do not meet these two exceptions, however, it is best to follow the aforementioned advice and stick to a clear, attractive, and easy-to-understand image. Save the fancier ones for your feed where they can be seen in a larger format and you can provide context for what it is that your followers are looking at.

Managing Important Instagram Settings

Instagram is designed with plenty of important settings that can support you in keeping your profile accessible and optimized to help you run your business. If you are using a business profile, there will be many additional settings that you can apply to your page in order to customize it even further. We will discuss that further in the next chapter.

In the meantime, here are the basic settings that you need to know about that come standard on every single profile:

Privacy Settings

On Instagram, everyone has the option of creating a private profile that potential followers must request to follow so that the owner of the account can approve all of their followers. For people who are seeking to keep themselves and their lives private, this can be a great way to keep yourself out of the eyes of strangers if you prefer to keep to yourself and stay private. For people who are building a brand, this is not a great idea.

Your profile will automatically have this privacy setting feature turned "off" and it is important that you leave it off. Having people unable to quickly see what you are all about and then have the option to follow you is going to result in you not having as many followers in the end. People do not like having to request to follow people they do not know as it can result in them feeling as though they are intruding on someone else's private space. Typically, they will simply skip the option and move on. That being said, there are still plenty of things that you can do to keep your account private from people who you may not want seeing your account, such as spammers or people who may be acting abusively on your page. Otherwise, the best (and most professional) practice is to make sure that you are not sharing any private images of yourself, your life, or your family that you would not want to have seen on the internet.

Two-Factor Authentication

Because you are building an empire, it is important that you take every precaution you can to avoid having that empire ruined by someone else. Hacking is a very real problem on virtually every social media platform, and unfortunately, it will likely always be a problem. That being said, social media platforms like Instagram are offering far more solutions to keep your account safe and protected so that this is not something you need to worry about. In order for you to access that fool-proof safety, however, you need to actually go into your settings and turn these features "on."

One feature you need to turn on is called "Two-Factor Authentication." You can turn this feature on by going into your Instagram settings, clicking the "Two-Factor Authentication" button and then following the prompts to turn this service on. You are going to want to do this as this will make logging into your account nearly impossible for any hacker who may be trying to hijack your account. With this service on, anytime someone logs into your account, including yourself, there will be a secondary step required in order to successfully log in. If it is you attempting to log in, this will be simple as it will just send a text message to your phone so that you can verify yourself using a code they will provide you with. If it is not you attempting to log in but instead it is someone attempting to hack you, this two-factor authentication feature will prevent them from gaining access because you will simply be able to block it from your phone.

Blocking Accounts

On Instagram, there tends to be a lot of spammers or "trolls" who will come out of the woodworks from time to time. They seem to come in waves, and they are not always a problem for everyone who spends time on Instagram. They tend to be worse if you use lower quality hashtags, such as #followforfollow or #likeforlike. These hashtags can quickly accumulate spammers on your account who are attempting to sell you on followers. Typically, their accounts offer followers in exchange for a certain amount of money. Which, by the way, is not a good idea because purchased followers can seriously hurt your visibility as you will learn more about in Chapter 5.

If you come across people who are spamming your account or who are even being abusive on your account such as through bullying, which can sometimes happen, you can easily deal with this by blocking said account. You should also take a moment to report their account so that Instagram recognizes that the account is being used inappropriately and can take action to prevent it from happening again. To do this, start by dragging the person's comment to the left on your device and then tap the "!" button on the slider. There, you can follow the process of reporting the inappropriate comment to Instagram so that the inappropriate account can be dealt with properly. Once you are done, you can click on that person's username to go to their Instagram account. From there, tap the three small dots in the top right corner and then tap "Block." Their account will now be both reported and blocked so they can no longer leave abusive or annoying comments on your posts. All you have to do now is go back to the original comment and delete it by sliding it to the left and tapping the red delete button!

Story Sharing Settings

The stories you create on Instagram can be shared on Facebook if you choose to link your accounts together. On your basic Instagram account, your profile can be linked to any Facebook profile or page. You can do this by going to your settings, tapping "Linked Accounts" and then "Facebook" and then choosing which account or page you want to link to your Instagram account. Once you have, you can go to your story settings and tap "Share To Facebook." With this feature on, every time you share a story to your Instagram story feed you will automatically have that same story shared into your Facebook story feed, too. This is a great opportunity to market on two platforms at the same time, so you should definitely consider turning this feature on and taking advantage of it.

* * *

Action Step: Build And Proof Your Profile

Now that you have all of the knowledge on what you need to do in order to build your profile, it is time for you to start creating! You should start by going to your internet browser, heading to Instagram and searching up some hashtags that are relevant to your niche. Then, you can take a peek at other Instagram profiles that are performing well on the platform. Pay attention to accounts that have more than 10,000 followers, that receive at least 300-400 likes on their photos, and seem to have many comments and engagement back and forth, too. This type of engagement shows that they are a high functioning account and that they are going to be effective accounts for you to follow and pay attention to.

As you are looking at these profiles, pay attention to what profile images, usernames, bios, and links they are using on their accounts. See what about their accounts are attractive, what you like, and what you feel is going to really work well with your brand and image. Getting a feel for how other accounts in your niche are working and what is helping them to succeed is going to give you the best opportunity to emulate that by mixing together all of your favorite pieces and producing your own unique profile. Once you have gathered enough inspiration you can simply follow the steps in this chapter and put together your own profile!

4 Building A Business Account

On Instagram, having a business account is not necessarily required even if you are going to be using Instagram for your business. Many businesses operate with basic accounts and see great success off of this approach. However, there are many benefits to having a branded account and there are many reasons as to why you may want to choose to turn yours into one. In this chapter, we are going to explore why business accounts are effective, what you can do with a business account, and why you might want to consider one. If you do decide that you want to have a business account, we are also going to discuss how you can convert your account over and what settings you need to know about in order to optimize your page.

The Benefits Of Instagram Business Accounts

There are a handful of reasons as to why brands are choosing to use business accounts on Instagram, including many additional features that come in handy when you are running a business on the platform. Two of the biggest reasons why business accounts are preferred is because they allow you to provide a location for your followers to see, as well as a call to action. If you are a local business, having your location displayed at the top of your profile can make it much easier for your potential clients to find you and begin visiting you in person. If you do not run a local business, such as if you have many locations, or if your business is entirely online you can always leave this information out to avoid confusing your followers. Having a call to action is also great because it offers a quick one-click feature for customers to get in touch with you so that they can learn more about your business.

Another major benefit to having your business account turned on is that your Instagram will begin tracking analytics on your page, posts, and link. Instagram's analytics will tell you about information such as how many followers you have grown by, what your most popular posting time is, what your most popular image is, and how many people are clicking through your links. They will also give you some information as to who your demographic is including what gender they are, what age range they fall under, and where they tend to be located. Having access to this type of information helps you determine whether your content is effectively reaching your targeted demographic or not. You can learn more about how to interpret and respond to these statistics in Chapter 11.

Finally, Instagram's business accounts have the added benefit of being able to run promotions and ads on the platform. If you have a business that you want to be running ads for, this is the only way to gain access to this feature which makes it well worth it for you to convert over. Basic profiles do not have access to this feature, so you will not be able to run promotions on your basic account if you do not convert over.

Converting To A Business Account

Converting from a basic account to a business account is extremely easy. Simply go to your accounts settings and tap "Switch To Business Account" and Instagram will walk you through a process of setting up your business account. In order to do so, you will need to set up a Facebook page which will be linked to the account as this provides Instagram with important information such as what category your business falls into. If you do not already have a page, Instagram will help you set one up quickly by switching you over to your Facebook application and walking you through the process. After you have completed it, you will be able to go back to your Instagram app and finish setting up your business account.

Note that if you do not already have a Facebook page and you need to make one for your Instagram creation, you are not necessarily required to begin promoting on your Facebook page immediately. You can always brand it, put up a few posts and then let it sit on the back burner as you master Instagram. Then, once you feel confident about your Instagram strategy you can start mastering your Facebook strategy so that you have two high functioning social media accounts. Alternatively, you can begin mastering both at the same time and using many of the handy cross-platform features that Facebook has conveniently built in for both applications, such as cross-promoting and cross-posting.

Determining Your Call to Action

Once you have set up your business account you are going to need to set up a call to action on your page. This call to action can be used to complete a few things, from quickly giving your followers direction to your store or bringing up an email so that they can send you a message. It is important that you use this button effectively so that whichever action your followers take is quick, easy, and makes sense with what you are attempting to achieve. For example, if your Instagram account is a funnel to get more people into your store, having directions to your physical location would be ideal here. If your Instagram account is a funnel for your online business, you may use this button to help people contact you.

Getting an action button on your profile does require you to link with a third party application, so you will need to be ready to prepare an account with any of the third parties listed on the Instagram partners tab. In order to find out more about who is included on this tab, you can go to your account settings, tap "Contact Options" then select "Add an Action Button." On that page, you will see an entire list of partners who you can connect to your Instagram account to achieve anything from booking tickets to ordering off of your menu if you are running a restaurant. If you see an action that you would like to take advantage of you can go into your web browser and create an account with that partner, and then go back to Instagram and tap that partner's name on the list and begin linking your accounts. You will need to go back to the partner site and fill in any necessary information to ensure that the feature works properly for your followers.

If you choose to use a partner and create an action button it is important that you choose an action button that makes sense to your business. For example, running a hair salon using a booking button would make plenty of sense; however, using a restaurant ordering feature would not. Exercise common sense here, consider what button is going to serve your followers the most, and consider how it fits into your sales funnel. If it makes sense and it will serve your customers well, you can easily plug in the steps above and get yourself a great funnel going!

Managing Important Business Account Settings

Instagram business accounts have added features that are intended to make them more effective and useful for the brands using these account formats. If you are using a business account you are going to want to know how you can modify these settings to ensure that you are getting the most out of your Instagram account. After all, if you are going to be putting in the time and money to get your account going you want to make sure that you are investing in all of the right ways! You want your investment to go far and help you get as many followers and conversions as possible, so make sure you are completely optimized to avoid missing out on anything due to a failure to launch on your end!

There are three primary settings that you need to pay attention to when it comes to building your Instagram business account. They are as follows:

Verifying Your Account

Some brands and public features have the capacity to get their branded account verified to prove to followers that the page is authentic and not someone trying to pretend to be another brand or public figure. If you are just starting your business, you may not be able to get your account verified. However, if you have been around for a while or you have a noteworthy business, getting your account verified may be a great idea to avoid having people confused by you versus anyone who may be pretending to be you.

In order to get your account verified, you have to request for Instagram to verify your account through your settings menu. You can do so by going to your settings, tapping "Account" and then "Request Verification." On that page, you will have the opportunity to fill out a form and send it to Instagram to be considered for verification. If you are approved, Instagram will message you back letting you know and they will add a blue check mark next to your name proving that you are a verified and legible account. This is a great way to help begin building trust in you and your brand, so if you are a larger brand it is a good idea to give this a try and see if Instagram would be willing to give you a verification mark.

Getting Approved For Shopping

Businesses who sell products may be eligible to sell their products on Instagram by offering unique product tags that help customers quickly shop for what they see in pictures with minimal effort. These tags work similarly to tagging other people in posts, except they are focused on helping people locate the products displayed in images. You will simply tag your products and have links connected to the product's page on your website so that followers can tap your image, click the tag and go to the product page so that they can purchase your products.

In order to be able to turn on shopping features, you must first be approved by Instagram as they do not want to have brands spamming their followers through this feature. To become approved, you will need to go to the Instagram website and take a look at the "Merchant Agreement" and "Commerce Policies." You will need to comply with both of these in order to be eligible for tagging products in your photographs. Then, you will need to produce a catalog on your Facebook page which can be done by going to your Facebook page heading into the settings, clicking the "Tabs" setting and adding a catalog. You will fill out your product catalog on Facebook before returning to Instagram to link your catalog to your Instagram account. Once it has been linked, you can begin tagging products directly in your images for easier shopping on your followers' behalf.

If you do sell products, you should seriously consider offering this feature for your followers. This makes shopping for your products quick and easy, which can help your followers stay focused and engaged in the purchasing process. Followers to have to head to your account, go to your link, find the product and then check out are less likely to go through with the process of purchasing. This gives them more time to lose interest or lose focus, potentially preventing them from finalizing the purchase at all. The quicker and easier the purchasing process is, the more likely people will actually purchase your products online.

Managing Your Messages

The last setting you need to consider when you are setting up your business page is your message settings. In your business inbox, you have the option of filtering out your messages so that it is easier for you to see everything sitting in your inbox. You can either choose the option of seeing your entire inbox or seeing only messages that have not yet been read or that have been starred so that you can reply to them again later such as when you are following up on something. It is important that you know how to use this as this can make keeping up with customers far easier than scrolling back in your inbox and trying to keep up with everything.

In order to filter your messages you simply need to tap the icon that features three lines with the three dots across them that is located on the right side of the search bar. Once you have tapped it, the three filtering options will pop up letting you decide what messages you want to see. Using these to your advantage by building a messaging system for yourself is extremely simple and will make keeping up with your inbox a breeze. Simply start using it by tapping "Unread" and then going through your inbox starting at the oldest unread message, which will be featured at the bottom of your inbox screen. Then, read and respond to the said message as you normally would. If that message is one that will need follow up or features something important that you will need to remember, simply star the message so that it is seen as a 'priority' message in your inbox. Every few days make sure that you go to your starred messages and go through them so that any follow up or important information is completed and nothing is forgotten. When the interaction has been completed you can deselect the star on the message so that it is no longer featured in your starred inbox. Using this type of system makes keeping up with your followers a breeze and prevents you from missing out on important information or forgetting to follow up with a potential customer and missing out on a sale.

* * *

Action Step: Optimizing Your Business Account

If you have decided that you want to develop a business account for yourself and take advantage of the features available for Instagram business accounts, now is the time for you to optimize your account! Simply make the switch and then follow the steps in this chapter to help you set up your account and optimize it for the best results.

Remember, if you are unsure about which feature are going to be most useful for you in your unique niche or category and you want to get some inspiration you can always turn to your competitors. Get an idea of what the trends are in your niche when it comes to action buttons, product catalogs, and location sharing and determine what is going to fit your needs and your followers' needs the best. Then, begin implementing these techniques so that you can optimize your business account profile!

5 Conquering The Instagram Algorithm

The Instagram algorithm is an ever-changing place as the developers seek to consistently turn it into an even more powerful, effective, and relevant platform to hang out on. All of the information that you will find in this chapter are relevant at the time of writing this, but adjustments may be made going forward. The best way to utilize this chapter and get the most out of it is to use it as a starting point in order to fully understand and comprehend the value and purpose of the algorithm. You will also discover how you can leverage the algorithm so that you can maximize your visibility and, of course, increase the return on your investment in terms of both time and money. As time goes on, this algorithm will adjust to help improve the platform so you will need to stay up to date by regularly checking in on any changes that may have been made. You can easily do this by looking up blogs that specialize in Instagram or social media marketing as they will regularly update you on the small changes being made. That being said, this chapter will give you the foundation of knowledge that you need so that as you educate yourself on these various changes they make sense and you can easily accommodate for them.

Learning algorithms can take some time, so it is important that you truly study this chapter and invest yourself in learning the algorithm. Once you understand it and how it works you will discover how you can leverage it so that you can maximize your growth. A lot of people tend to grow frustrated with algorithm changes and may spread misinformation about how Instagram is attempting to censor people and "shadow banning" of accounts. In other words, they believe that Instagram is preventing their posts from getting seen because they are not getting enough interaction or engagement to make it seem like their efforts are actually working. Typically, what is actually happening is that said person is not aware of how the algorithm works so they are failing to create traction with their account. I would suggest avoiding these types of blogs that spread such misinformation as it will only lead to you feeling frustrated and struggling to produce results. Instead, look for information that is based on driving results and helping you create success as these are the platforms that are actually educated and that will give you tips that will work in helping you stay visible.

The Value Of The Algorithm

Algorithms are often talked about as though they are a form of censorship when in reality, they are actually a highly valuable tool when it comes to social media. On social media, the algorithms are designed to help you see only the people that you are most likely to be interested in. This means that you are unlikely to see everyone you follow in your feed, but instead, you are going to see people who you follow *and* interact with on a regular basis. When advertisements or sponsored posts pop up, these will also include content that is relevant to what you have been looking at, who you follow, or what content you have been engaging with on your own profile. The idea behind this is that sites like Instagram want to ensure that your entire feed is curated of content that you are actually going to like. By doing this, they can keep your newsfeed interesting and relevant to your interests and help you stay engaged. To them, this makes you far more likely to actually come back and continue using their platform because you are actually interested in the content you are seeing.

If the algorithm were not to exist, you would see so many different posts that it may be hard to actually keep up with anyone. Furthermore, you would likely be seeing a lot of content that you are not actually interested in. For example, say you follow various members of your family because you are related but you are not entirely interested in everything that they post. If the algorithm was not in place, your news feed would still be filled with these posts and you may find yourself growing bored or disinterested in the platform because the information was redundant or irrelevant to what you are interested in. With the algorithm in place, you do not have this problem because everything you are being shown is actually relevant to what you are interested in seeing.

Algorithms exist everywhere, on virtually every website or social media platform that you have ever been on or used. These algorithms are in place for various things to happen, from helping you see content that is more appropriate to your interests to helping the website host have an idea of what people are actually interested in seeing. They are not intended to create censorship or take away from your experience on social media but instead, they are designed to help you see only what you are actually interested in. That way, your experience is personalized and enjoyable and you are far more likely to come back and engage with your friends and followers on their platform.

How The Instagram Algorithm Works

The Instagram algorithm is based on three signals: interest, timeliness, and relationship. By paying attention to how your interactions on their platform measure in terms of these three signals, the algorithm is able to calculate what you are most likely to be interested in and share relevant content with you. It also pays attention to how your content is rating in terms of interest, timeliness, and relationship and using this information to decide who is going to see your content. If you are using the platform correctly and leveraging the algorithm, you will be excelling in these three areas which means you will be far more likely to have engagement on your content.

Let us take a deeper look at what these signals are and how Instagram uses them to curate your newsfeed, as well as your followers' newsfeeds.

Interest

Instagram wants to see how likely you are to care about a post that someone else has posted. If they think that you will "like" the post, then it will appear on your timeline for you to see. The posts that Instagram thinks you will like the most will appear higher in your feed whereas the ones that Instagram thinks you will be less likely to enjoy will appear lower in your feed. While they are still there, it takes significantly longer to actually get to them.

The way that Instagram is able to gauge how much you will like a post is by paying attention to your previous interactions and engagements on the platform. Instagram will track what types of hashtags you are following, what keywords are most present in the captions, and who the account belongs to. If you tend to like several pictures that all share similar hashtags or captions, or if you are consistently liking content by the same people, Instagram is going to determine that you are interested in these topics or people and push them up higher in your newsfeed. For the content that you do not like as much or that you don't like at all, Instagram will push it lower in your newsfeed or not show it at all to avoid creating a newsfeed that is uninteresting to you.

A good way to determine how the interest aspect of the algorithm is working for you at this time is to take a look at your Instagram Explore Page. You can find this page by tapping the search button in your actions bar at the bottom of the application. There, you will find several different posts that Instagram believes are relevant to what you are interested in. If you simply 'like' everything without actually being interested in it, this discovery page will likely look very confusing and will feature several different types of content. If you only 'like' the things that actually interest you, however, this discovery page will be perfectly curated of content that Instagram believes you will be most interested in, regardless of whether or not you actually follow the accounts being shown.

For your followers, the more you can get them to 'like' your posts or comment on them, the more Instagram will see them as interested and the higher up you will be in their newsfeeds. As a result, you will consistently get higher and higher engagement and you will have an easier time retaining your current followers and gaining new ones.

Timeliness

Instagram's current algorithm is designed to show more recent photographs, rather than ones that may be extremely old or out of date. As a result, you are less likely to see posts from over a week ago. In addition to when posts were made, Instagram also determines how often the post is being liked or engaged with. If people are interacting with your posts quickly and it accumulates many likes over a shorter period of time, you will be driven further up in other people's newsfeeds, too. You will also be more likely to show up on their discovery pages if you align with what they are actively interested in. If your posts are not engaged with quickly or it takes a long time for them to accumulate interest, your post will be less likely to show up in the newsfeed or discovery pages meaning it will be even harder to gain interest.

In order to really drive up your engagement, there are some different strategies that you can use. Scheduling your posts, using relevant hashtags, sharing high-quality images, and using effective keywords and captions are all excellent ways to increase your engagement and drive yourself further up in the algorithm. We will discuss these strategies in greater detail later on.

Relationship

The last thing Instagram will be paying attention to is your relationship to the people that you are engaging with. If you are continually commenting on one person's photos or if you are being tagged in their content on a regular basis, Instagram is going to consider these people to be closer to you. Because of this, they will start showing up more in your newsfeed and you will be able to continue seeing them and engaging with them on a more regular basis.

The best way to use relationship to your advantage is to go to people's accounts and actually comment on their stuff. Ideally, you should comment on three or more of their pictures as this will cue the algorithm as well as have that person paying attention. Comments are far more likely to capture user's attention over likes, and while one is a great way to capture someone's attention two or three shows that you are actually interested and spending time on their account. As a result, they are going to be more likely to reciprocate the interest and check out your account. If you are someone they may be interested in following, then you can earn a follow from their account and potentially increase your engagement, popularity, and conversion ratios.

* * *

Action Step: Leveraging The Algorithm

There are many ways for you to leverage the Instagram algorithm, but the most effective ways are to consider these three signals every single time you post on your account. By showing interest in people's content and increasing their interest in yours, being timely by posting frequently and receiving engagement quickly, and by cultivating relationships with people on Instagram you can maximize your visibility.

The rest of this book is going to be devoted to discussing the very practices that can help you increase your interest, timeliness, and relationships so the best way for you to discover how to master the algorithm is to read on to the next chapters. Keep the algorithm in mind as you read so that you can begin to understand how Instagram works, why these strategies are effective, and how you can really make them work for you. That way as you customize your strategy you are not accidentally customizing it in a way that takes away from your ability to leverage the algorithm and experience massive growth with less frustration.

6 Designing Your Content

Now that you have all of the underlying pieces and knowledge in place, it's time for you to start strategizing your marketing approach! Designing your Instagram content properly is vital if you want to have it set up in a way that is going to be attractive, informative, and effective in converting followers to clients. There are a few things that go into designing your content in a way that is going to promote engagement so that you can boost your visibility in the Instagram algorithm. Which approach you use will largely depend on who your target audience is, though there are some basic strategies that are going to help you determine exactly what approach you need.

In this chapter, we are going to begin by identifying what your posting schedule should look like, what types of strategies you need to build into your schedule, and how you can leverage it for maximum effectiveness. This will be the basis of your content strategy, allowing you to identify what you are going to be posting and when. In the next chapter, we will go into greater detail about specific post types and how you can leverage them to optimize your content strategy.

Understanding Content Strategy

If you are new to marketing, content strategies may be somewhat foreign to you. Essentially, content strategies are strategies that you put together that state when you are going to post, how often, and what that post will contain. By creating an effective strategy you can build a profile that is attractive and informative, thus increasing your conversion ratios and helping you get the most out of your time investment on Instagram.

On Instagram specifically, there are four things that you need to be aware of when it comes to developing a posting strategy. The first thing you need to be aware of is a schedule that is going to tell you what days you need to be posting on your Instagram, and at what time you need to be posting them. You also need to consider what your objectives are so that you know what type of posts you need to be making and when. Then, you need to consider how often you are going to propose a pitch or a call to action in your content so that you how often you are actually going to be asking for sales. Lastly, you need to come up with a strategy for how you are going to handle user-generated content and how you will leverage it to maximize your sales.

Developing A Posting Schedule

One of the signals in Instagram's algorithm is "timeliness" which refers to both how quickly your post generates interest, and how often you are posting. In order to leverage the algorithm and increase your engagement, you need to be using a posting schedule that will ensure that you remain active and consistent in generating content from your profile. Building a content calendar is going to help you decide which days to post, how many times to post, and what times you should be posting at for maximum engagement. That being said, you are going to need to do some research to determine which exact strategy is going to help leverage you in your unique business. Each target audience will have slightly different time frames as to when they are on Instagram and what they are doing on Instagram. For example, an audience who works in an office from 9-5 may be unlikely to go on Instagram until the evening, whereas entrepreneurs who run their businesses online are likely to check in intermittently throughout the day. Spending some time researching your audience and generating a backlog of analytics surrounding this information will ensure that you are choosing posting times that are going to help you maximize engagement and get seen. The best way to build up a backlog of analytics is to spend a couple of weeks practicing posting at different times each day, and posting in different volumes. For example, on some days you may just post once and you may change that one post from morning to noon to night time, whereas other days you might post three times at different intervals. Playing around like this for a couple of weeks will give your Instagram analytics enough information to start generating accurate results for you based on when your best posting times are.

Once you have a backlog of analytics information you can begin developing your content calendar. This calendar should state what you are going to post and when so that you have a clear objective when you go into marketing on your account. This should include how many times per day, which days, what times, and what exact content you are going to be posting at each time. If you will be doing any sales or highlighting specific topics in your business at different times you should be highlighting this in your content calendar, too. For example, if you are running a Black Friday sale you should be writing in "black Friday sale" on your content calendar for each day that the sale will be on and that you will be posting. That way, you know exactly what to post and you can keep your objective clear and focused.

If you are looking for a great tool to help you with scheduling, I highly recommend checking out Hootsuite (https://hootsuite.com/). This platform is great for managing not only Instagram but all of your other social media accounts as well. The entire purpose of the platform is for you to be able to manage your social media accounts in one local area, making it far easier for you to stay consistent and track your progress around the net.

Choosing Your Marketing Objectives

On the topic of objectives, you should always have very clear objectives when it comes to developing a content strategy for your Instagram page. You want to make sure that everything you post has a clear objective outlined before you even begin writing the post so that you can help your business forward in achieving your goals. Your objectives should always align with your larger goals so that you can start moving forward effectively. For example, say you are setting the goal to earn a certain amount of increased traffic to your website each month through Instagram. You should then have objectives that relate to building engagement, developing relationships with your followers, and directing them to your website link.

Every single post should fall under these categories to ensure that you are always working towards your goal, as well as to help you measure your success. So, say you try a new marketing strategy such as using different words, describing emotions, asking questions, or something else that is new. If you had an objective outlined for your post to "increase engagement" you would be able to clearly determine whether or not that specific strategy was working for you based on how much engagement you received on that picture. That way, you can decide whether it is a strategy that you can continue using or if you need to adjust it or change it in order to maximize your effectiveness.

Creating A Pitch Ratio

The last part of your content calendar that you need to consider is your pitch ratio. You need to determine how often you are going to make a clear pitch to your audience, either by letting them know about a sale or a product or encouraging them to go to your website to "learn more." Ideally, your ratio should be around 10-20% pitches and 80-90% building engagement and letting people know who you are, what your mission is, and how you can help them. Although this may seem rather low, only making actual pitches 10-20% of the time will increase your engagement and the number of people who are clicking through to your website. This is because your other posts are generating genuine interest which then encourages people to make the effort to go learn more about you on their own account. Since they came up with the idea to look on their own, they are more likely to remain interested and actually follow through on making a purchase than someone who has been directly told to.

On Instagram, your goal is to generate interest and encourage click-throughs, not to specifically tell people to purchase your stuff. Your pitch posts should be more of a reminder or a heads up than a specific pitch to ensure that you come across as genuine and interesting. Creating too many pitches will result in people thinking that you are spammy or that you do not have a genuine interest in building up a reputation and generating relationships with your clients. As a result, they will unfollow you and you will lose traction in your business really fast. Instagram is all about nurturing relationships and showing off inspiring, informational, or exciting content. If you stick primarily to those three areas then you will do great at generating more interest in your business and turning higher conversions through your page.

In order to help you get a feel for what the pitch ratio looks like online, I encourage you to follow people who are using it effectively on their own accounts. This way, you can see it in action and feel inspired to master your own pitch ratio as well.

Some great accounts to follow for inspiration include:

- Gary Vaynerchuk at *@garyvee*
- Robert Kiyosaki at *@therealkiyosaki*
- Echo Summer Hill at *@echosummerhill*
- Amanda Frances at *@xoamandafrances*
- Tony Robbins at *@tonyrobbins*
- Adidas at *@adidas*

User-Generated Content Strategies

As you begin developing a larger following and generating sales through your Instagram account you are likely going to start experiencing the development of user-generated content. This is content that other people share that feature your products and have you tagged in the content. When this begins to happen, you can begin producing a user-generated content strategy to support you in leveraging this content so that you can start getting even further with your Instagram strategy.

User-generated content is particularly special because this content is designed by someone other than your own brand and typically sings your praise. As a result, these types of posts generate what is known as "social proof" or evidence that other people are purchasing your products and actively enjoying them. By having these posts on Instagram, you are gaining access to other people touting your praise and letting people know that they are likely going to enjoy and appreciate both your content and your products. In other words, this is a great marketing strategy that gets you in front of a whole slew of brand new eyes.

User-generated content can be organic, or it can be encouraged. Some brands will create unique hashtags that are used by their audience when tagging their brand to help them promote their business. These movements' are simple to start and can really help you build a lot of traction in your business by creating a community of people who are all talking about your products and services. They also allow new potential clients to look at your hashtag and discover that there are several other people that are a part of your community who are enjoying your products. You can also encourage user-generated content through hosting contests, giveaways, and other incentive-based marketing strategies on your page.

If you are unsure about how you can leverage user-generated content to the fullest, I recommend checking out some of the popular brands that are already doing it. Some of these brands include: Dove (*@dove*), Nike Run Club (*@nikerunning*), KitKat (*@kitkat*), and Starbucks (*@starbucks*).

Once you begin developing user-generated content, you can start using it to help promote your business even further. For example, you can ask for the permission of the person who posted the original image and then repost their image on your own profile. There, you can make a comment about how much they are loving your products, thank them for the lovely picture, and then tag the user who originally posted said image with your products. Actions like this help you not only leverage their content but also shine a spotlight on your clients who are willingly praising you on the internet, thus helping them feel special and making them more likely to continue supporting you and promoting you amongst their friends.

* * *

Action Step: Develop Your Strategy

Now that you know everything that goes into developing a strategy for Instagram, it is time for you to begin actually creating one! You are going to do so by creating a content calendar and determining when you are going to post, what, and when. As you do, I encourage you to set up your first two weeks' worth of content in a way that tests what times are best for posting and what volumes as well. A good idea would be to have each day set up where you post at different times between one and three times per day. Make sure that you get a good variety so that Instagram has plenty of information to use in order to begin producing accurate analytics. Once you have done two full weeks this way you should know exactly when your best posting times are throughout the week. Then, you can determine your volume and create your content calendar based on the number of posts you will make and when.

Once you have the basic structure of your content calendar in place, you can begin testing with different strategies to help you determine which strategies work the best for your platform. Ideally, you should enforce one new strategy per week or three to four new strategies per month to see what works the best on your platform. That way, you generate plenty of data around each strategy to help you determine whether or not it is working. If part way through the calendar you realize it is not working it's best you can always make small tweaks and adjustments to see if you can improve it and produce a strategy that works effectively. If not, you can switch to a new strategy in the following week.

7 Understanding Content and Themes

Now that you understand the purpose of content and how you can develop a content strategy that is going to work for you when it comes to designing your approach, you need to start understanding content and themes! On Instagram, there are three different areas where you can post and multiple different types of contents and themes that you can employ on your page. In this chapter, we are going to explore where you can post online, what types of content you should be generating, and what themes you should be implementing. This will help you get a better idea of specific strategies that you can enforce alongside your general marketing strategy to help you experience great success on your page.

Places To Post

Instagram offers three unique areas for you to post content. You will want to be regularly taking advantage of each area so that you are creating plenty of content for your followers to pay attention to. If you really want to take your content game to the next level, creating a content calendar for each of these avenues can support you in making sure that you are regularly providing excellent content for your followers to enjoy.

On Your Feed

On your Instagram feed is where you are going to be curating a visible profile for people to see and visit on a regular basis. Here, you are going to want to be generating a 'look' that is well-curated, makes sense, and is attractive enough to keep people on your page long enough to see what you are all about.

Your feed will include images, captions, and hashtags to attract people to visit your profile. You should be posting around 1-3 times per day in order to make sure that you are staying active enough to be seen by people who are hanging out on Instagram. It should be designed in a way that features a clear theme and that has content that is inspirational, educational, entertaining, or actionable.

On Your Stories

Your Instagram stories allow for you to share the 'behind-the-scenes' of your life or your business with your followers so that they can see more of what you are doing beyond your page. Stories are only shared for 24 hours before they disappear forever unless you pin them as a 'highlight' which allows them to be featured on your page until you decide to remove them. Another feature that is built into your stories is known as 'live video' which allows you to share real-time video clips with your audience so that they can engage with you right then and there.

On your stories, you can be more flexible with your look because you are not curating a feed that needs to be attractive and interesting. While you still want the content to be high quality and relevant, you can be more flexible in what you are posting and what it looks like to your followers. You should be uploading to your stories multiple times per day so that your audience has plenty of intimate and exclusive content to look at what keeps them feeling personally connected to your brand.

On Your IGTV Channel

Instagram recently released a platform known as "IGTV" which is built directly into the Instagram platform and can be found on your home page. IGTV is designed to allow you to take videos with your phone and then share them on your channel for as long as you desire so that your audience has more to watch. In a sense, this is like a form of YouTube that has been built directly into Instagram so that your followers can watch your videos and learn more from you through your channel. You should be uploading at least once a week or, at the very least, once or twice a month to ensure that there is some form of content here for your followers to engage with.

Types Of Content

There are many different types of content that you could be uploading onto your profile to keep your page well-rounded, interesting, and attractive to your audience. Getting lazy in the types of content that you are posting can result in your audience growing bored and no longer wanting to follow you or your page anymore. This is the exact opposite of what you want happening, so you will want to make sure that you include many different types of content into your strategy. Not every brand is going to make sense with all types of content, so pick 4-5 that would fit your image and use those as a way to create an interesting and diverse profile that stays entertaining and relevant for your audience.

Inspirational Content

Inspirational content is a great sharing opportunity for virtually any brand to take advantage of. Inspirational content is uplifting, empowering, and enjoying to pay attention to. People love reading or seeing something that makes them feel good inside or that reminds them that they are wonderful, worthy, and capable human beings. There are many different ways that you can incorporate inspirational content into your strategy so make sure you take the time to understand your audience's needs and then start going from there.

Some examples of inspiring content you can share include sharing an inspiring quote, write a caption that is filled with inspiration, or uploading an nspirational video to your story or to your IGTV channel. The inspiration that you share should be relevant to your overall message in some way so that your audience understands it. For example, if you are a clothing brand you will want to be sharing inspirational content about things like body positivity, feeling confident in wearing your favorite clothes, and inner beauty, *not* about things like food, animals, or other unrelated topics. The only exception would be if your clothing brand somehow ties in with another industry, such as if a portion of your proceeds are donated to an animal charity.

Human Faces

Human faces are said to generate far more engagement on your profile because they are relatable and interesting. When people see human faces on your profile they begin to develop a feeling inside that mirrors a relationship, thus helping them feel as though they are building a relationship directly with your brand. As a result, this personal connection can help cultivate brand loyalty, memorable content, and an interest that is often strong enough to inspire people to check out your profile and see what you have to offer.

Using human faces also gives you the opportunity to express things that basic images may not be able to. For example, human faces have the capacity to 'say' things through facial expressions that still-shots of products or landscaping simply cannot convey. Taking the time to actually capture photographs of human faces, such as yours, that 'say' what you want your message to say to the other person helps generate content that is interesting, relatable, and inspiring. There are countless ways that you can incorporate human faces into your marketing strategy so get creative and have fun with this.

Landscapes and Scenery

Despite not being as relatable as human faces, landscapes and scenery are known to be highly popular on Instagram because they can inspire feelings of peace, curiosity, and happiness in the people who are looking at said photographs. Travel accounts are extremely popular because they tend to display several pictures of landscapes and sceneries that are vastly different from the typical scenes that most people see on a day to day basis. Because they are so different and unique, people become inspired and feel dreamy and wonderous when they look at these pictures, which inspires them to engage and follow the account posting these images.

Even if you are not a travel blog, there are often still many ways that you can incorporate landscapes and scenery into your images so that you can inspire these feelings of happiness and curiosity in your followers, too. A great example would be taking an image where a beautiful piece of landscaping is in the background, such as taking a selfie in front of the Grand Canyon or shooting a fashionable image of your outfit with gorgeous gardens behind you. Incorporating landscaping and scenery into your images helps add depth to your profile and your pictures so don't be afraid to get creative and incorporate interesting backgrounds with multiple layers into your feed.

Food Pictures

Food pictures have a tendency to go over really well on Instagram, particularly if they are high-quality pictures of dishes that have been elegantly prepared. The food industry has a great foothold on the Instagram platform as this offers restaurants, food critics, and other self-proclaimed foodies the opportunity to share images of their food with people. Images of food tend to be far more interesting and captivating than mere descriptions, which makes Instagram highly effective when it comes to sharing your food photographs with people in the Instagram space.

Not every account is going to be able to share food images because these tend to be very niche-specific. For example, a clothing brand is likely not going to be able to seamlessly incorporate pictures of their meals because it simply does not make sense to the primary content being shared by the profile. If your account does work well with food, however, sharing high-quality images of dishes that have been well-designed is a great form of content that tends to get massive amounts of engagement.

You can also take food sharing one step further, particularly if you are a nutritionist or a personal trainer. Sharing your food images can be a great opportunity for you to caption them with a recipe, the nutritional content of the recipe, or other important nutrition-related information that your followers may need to know. This way, you are both educating your followers and sharing content that they are actively interested in paying attention to.

Action Pictures

Action pictures are images of you actively engaging with your products or in your services and sharing them with your followers. For example, if you are a yoga instructor you may share an image of you doing yoga or leading a class of other people who are doing yoga. If you are selling a unique product, you might share an image of you actively using the product and have it captioned with something relevant to the product itself.

Taking action pictures is a great opportunity to inspire people to think about what your product or service would be like *in action.* As a result, they are far more likely to feel interested in learning more because they can clearly visualize themselves using your products or services in their own life. You can also describe the action in the caption in a way that inspires them to further visualize themselves as engaging in said action, which can further increase their personal interest in your company.

Historical Pictures

Although you might not think it, people are actually fascinated by history and tend to be very curious about learning more about historical societies. Plus, history can come alongside a vintage or retro feel that often has people thinking about 'the good old days.' Sharing historical pictures on your page can be a great way to stimulate positive memories, educate people on the history of your brand, or introduce them to important information that somehow supports your brand's objective.

When you are sharing historical pictures, make sure that you are clear about what you are sharing and how it compares to your objective. For example, if you are sharing a historical picture of your brand from the day your business was incorporated or from another important part of your history, be clear as to what your audience is looking at. Let them know that they are seeing a piece of your brand's history that was monumental in helping you get to where you are now, and don't be afraid to include some inspiring content here to really help amplify the message behind your image. Or, you might share a historical image of the town where you originated in and discuss how far things have come and how proud you are to be a part of that town and why it is so important to you and your brand. How or if you incorporate history into your brand is ultimately going to depend on what your brand is about and how that history may support you in marketing yourself and inspiring your audience to reminisce on the past in some way.

Educational Content

Educational content is a great way for you to develop content that actually informs your audience as to what is important when it comes to your particular niche. For example, as a financial advisor, you might educate your audience on latest developments in the financial industry or inform them on important information about how they can manage and reduce their personal debt or build their personal equity. As a nutritionist, you might educate your audience about the importance of macronutrients or about how their hormones are impacted by food and how they can balance their hormones through their diet. Educational content like this is interesting to your audience which results in them wanting to continue following you because they are curious to learn more about what you are teaching them. It also positions you as the expert in your industry which leaves your audience thinking about you and your brand any time they want to learn more or gain something from your industry because they can trust that you know what you are talking about.

Educational content should be one of the most commonly used content types in your business. This type of content can be used in every single industry and for many different reasons. It can also be generated in many ways so that your wisdom drops don't become mundane, repetitive, or annoying to your audience. That way, they are excited and fascinated by all of the fresh and new information that you are bringing to light for them on a day to day basis.

Behind-the-Scenes Snapshots

Your audience does not want to feel like they are being alienated by you by having you hide certain aspects of your business or highly censor everything that you are sharing. Individuals, especially on Instagram, are rapidly moving towards supporting local businesses and getting to know the people who are behind the businesses that they are supporting. Attempting to hide your face or keep your business overly polished and censored can result in people thinking that you have something to hide or that you are not authentic or genuine. As a result, they will struggle to develop a relationship with you and your brand and they will be more likely to head elsewhere to gain information about your industry.

Building a behind-the-scenes 'image' on your Instagram is important as it gives your audience the opportunity to feel like they are special to you. By bringing them into the back-end operations of your business and life (to a degree) you can share a more genuine connection with your audience that leaves them honestly caring about you and your brand. While you do not want to be getting unprofessional or sharing overly intimate content here, bringing your audience behind the scenes to see things that clients do not typically see is powerful. You can share things such as what you do in your spare time, what you are passionate about, your family, the relationships shared by your coworkers, or any other 'private' information that is still in some way relevant to your business. Keeping your intimate relationship with your fans still somewhat curated ensures that your audience feels special but your image is still maintained and clear.

Real-Time Trends

Although trends are often short-lived, getting on board with them can be a great way to tap into the power of real-time trends and the sheer mass of interest that they can develop in a short amount of time. On Instagram, trends tend to rise and fall within a few days or weeks at a time. Getting involved in these trends and finding your own unique way to approach them and incorporate them into your business is a great opportunity for you to 'get on the bandwagon' and begin gaining traction and interest from trends.

It is important if you are going to partake in trends that you are paying close attention to the lifespan of the trend. You do not want to be posting trending content long after the trend has died off or you will become seen as irrelevant and outdated. This can result in people not wanting to follow you anymore because it feels like you are too behind on what is going on in your own industry. As a result, you may end up losing followers if you do not take the cue and hop off of the trend before it completely dies out. Make sure that if you are leveraging trending content that you are using it to stay relevant and that you are not hurting yourself through it.

Video Content

Video marketing is becoming a massive opportunity for brands to connect with their audiences, build face to face relationships, and develop an interactive face for their brands. Using video to market to your audience can be done in almost any manner, the options are truly limitless. You can use video content to inspire, uplift, and motivate your audience or you can use it to educate and inform them. Many people also use video content to create entertaining content for their followers to enjoy as they aspire to help their users laugh more or feel a sense of joy or fulfillment within.

You can use video marketing in many ways on Instagram. The IGTV and Instagram Live Video features are both designed to help you create video content and share it with your audience. You can also produce small clips that are 60 seconds or less to share on your page, or small 30 second clips to share in your stories. Make sure that, as with any other form of content, your videos make sense to your overall message and image. As well, be sure to use them in a diversified manner too so that you can share plenty of types of content via. video on your platform.

Types of Themes

On Instagram, many brands use themes as an opportunity to curate a specific image on their newsfeed. Themes can be based on the type of content being shared, the focal point in the images, the colors, or any other number of things. In this section, we are going to explore 10 different themes that are commonly used and how you can adjust them to suit your brand.

Moody Themes

Moody themes include any theme that inspires a certain mood or emotion in the people who are looking at the feed. You can create a theme that is bright and cheery, dark and romantic, or even deep and sultry. There are many different moods that you can invoke through imagery, so be creative if you are going to be inspired through moods. Really get a feel for what mood you want people to associate your brand with and leverage that through the posts that you share.

Creative Themes

Creative themes are ones that have a certain artistic appearance to them that is 'unusual' compared to the average theme. They may focus on certain colors, images, or designs to help create an overall aesthetic that is carried on across many pictures. Rather than simply having similar colors and focal points throughout their images, creative themes tend to attempt to create one large spectacle out of all of the images put together in the feed. Some examples of creative themes include rotating between different themes every so often, or using what is known as a "bordered" theme by adding a white or colored border to every single photograph before uploading it. Both of these will add a unique and creative element to your page, helping it stand out from the rest of the pages people are looking at on a daily basis.

Color-based Themes

Color-based themes are designed based on specific color palettes and seek to create an aesthetic that revolves around those colors. Color-based themes will always use images that feature the same color palette, making them flow together extremely well. You can design a color-based theme by using black and white photographs, color blocking your pictures, or having every single picture focused on incorporating a certain color palette such as pastels or jewel tones. These types of themes tend to be highly attractive because each picture looks so good on its own while also working well with your overall theme to produce a larger attractive image. Essentially, it turns your entire page into an ongoing work of art that you add to every single time you upload a new photograph to your page.

* * *

Action Step: Choose Your Look

Now that you know what themes are available and what type of content is considered popular on Instagram, it is time for you to decide what your look will be! Although your look is somewhat up to you, you also want to make sure that you choose a look that will be relevant to your audience. You do not want to use an image that is going to drive your target audience away for being too irrelevant to what they consider to be interesting or attractive. Instead, you want to create one that is going to lure them to your page and keep them wanting to interact with and engage with you.

The best way to choose your look is to consider what themes and looks your competitors are going for, as well as the ones that are being used by your audience. Creating a theme that reflects brands they already like while also somewhat mirroring your followers themselves ensures that you create an image that is actually interesting and attractive to your followers. Once you have your theme identified, you can simply plug in your own colors and brand feel to it so that you can customize it, thus allowing you to have a theme that is guaranteed to win while also being personalized and unique to you.

8 Ten Steps to Create The Perfect Instagram Post

In addition to creating the perfect feed, you also need to create the perfect Instagram post! Here are ten great steps for you to start using so that you can generate a great post every single time.

Step 1: Plan Your Image Wisely

Your image needs to make sense to your overall feed, as well as to the message that you want to share with your audience. Make sure that you get a feel for what images will accurately help reflect your message and take your photographs accordingly. For example, if you want to write about the value of getting your heart rate up during your workout consider choosing an image associated with cardio rather than one of a person who is just sitting down taking a drink. Your image should make sense to the message that you are sharing so that they both work together to amplify the posts purpose.

Step 2: Take Your Image

When you take your images for Instagram, seek to produce high quality images that people are actually going to be attracted to. Instagram is all about photo sharing, which means that people are highly competitive in not only their content but the quality of their photographs and content, too. You want your pictures to have a competitive edge by using the right lighting, the right poses, and the right colors to produce an attractive image overall.

Step 3: Edit Your Image

Most Instagram pictures are edited in one way or another. Editing images ensures that they are of the highest quality and that they are going to work together in your feeds overall look. Some great applications that you can use include FaceTune and Lightroom CC, both of which are available on your phone. These can help you turn a good image into a great image and really step up the quality of your Instagram game.

Step 4: Fit The Image Into Your Feed

Before you post the image, make sure that it is going to look appropriate next to all of your other images. Be mindful of what posts your new post is going to be next to and how it compliments them. If you really want to have a high quality feed, you need all of your images to tie in together to create a story, which is accomplished through mindful posting! You can use an Instagram feed planning tool like UNUM, which let's you slot in future content into your feed to see which images look best together.

Step 5: Tell Your Story

Once you have your image put together, you need to post your caption. On Instagram, shorter captions tend to be read by more people so keeping the majority of your captions shorter is ideal in order to increase your readership. However, longer posts do also have a tendency to connect better with your hot leads as it provides more value to them and gives them a better feel for your brand and what you stand for. I recommend combining the two by providing immediate value in the first sentence or two and then adding more in-depth information for those who care to read further. That way, you can appeal to both types of Instagram scrollers which will help you get more momentum towards your primary objective, whatever that may be!

Step 6: Use Your Caption Hashtags

In your caption, you can include a few hashtags either to highlight a specific message or simply to tag something relevant in the caption. However, you do not want to be using too many hashtags in your captions as this can look tacky and overwhelming and will result in no one reading your post.

Here are two great examples of how you can use hashtags directly in the post:

- *I absolutely #love this new #yoga bag I purchased last night!*
- *I absolutely love this new yoga bag I purchased last night! #yogimama #yogateacher*

Step 7: Create Your Hashtag Cluster

Only using one or two hashtags is not going to earn you much in terms of viewership, so you will need to also include a hashtag cluster in your post. You can either insert several enter spaces and post the hashtag cluster deep into the bottom of your main caption, or you can post your hashtag cluster into the first comment of your new post. I recommend using your first comment for this as it looks cleaner and it keeps it away from your beautiful caption. In order to make sure that you still maintain the same amount of momentum, you will want to pre-create your hashtag cluster and post it within the first 5 seconds of your new post being published. You can easily do this in a fresh note on your phone, or using an app like PLANN which will help you choose the best hashtags for your post.

Step 8: Include A Call To Action

In your main caption, you may want to include a call to action particularly if you are presently posting a pitch post. Your call to action should be brief and direct so that it does not take up too much of your readers time or attention. Lengthy call to actions will be ignored, which will result in them being a complete waste of your time and drive you in the opposite direction of your Instagram goals. Instead, try something short and simple like:

- *Do you love this new blazer as much as we do? Check out all of our colors on our website! Link in bio!*

- *Winter is upon us, equip yourself with everything you need to ditch the stress on our new Holiday page. Link in the bio.*
- *Don't you love these shoes? Go grab some! #linkinthebio*

Step 9: Partner Up With Influencers

If you are going to be leveraging influencers to grow your brand and they are in some way connected to your post, make sure that you are tagging those influencers in the post. Alternatively, you may put a call to action in your post that invites influencers to team up with your company. Make sure that this is clear so that your audience knows you are talking to them.

Step 10: Posts With Purpose

When you are posting for the purpose of promotional content, do not be afraid to use posts with a purpose. These posts have a deeper meaning that encourages your audience to pay attention by giving them a clear sense of what value they are going to gain from the post itself.

Some examples of posts with a purpose include:

- Carousel posts. Essentially, you post several images of products for sale and encourage your audience to swipe through to see all of your new or highlighted products. A great example of a popular company who uses this method is Sephora, who often highlights their weekly deals on a carousel reel.

- IG Story invites. If you have an event going on, invite people to join your event through your story feed. This is a fun way to offer a personalized invite and it feels more special to your audience than an in-feed post. Plus, it can keep your newsfeed free from tacky invitation style posts. Many celebrity rewards shows will use this method to invite people to the exclusive night.

- Do a Q&A with IGTV live/Channel. You can easily go live or prerecord a video and do a Q&A either directly with your audience, or by interviewing someone who your audience admires. Many different life coaches are presently using this as an opportunity to provide added value to their followers.

- Run promotions and discounts in your story. Many boutique-style stores use their stories as a way to run promotions and get them directly to their audience without crowding up their feed. A great example of this is @prairiebazaar who uses their story to sell their vintage home decor items without overwhelming their feed.

- Create ad reels using Instagram Video. Companies like Nike are using short video clips to highlight new products or sales on their Instagram profiles. These short video clips are a great way to get your sales out there in an attractive and totally relevant way, since video advertising is currently rising in popularity!

Instagram Resource Cheat Sheet

The following resources are great tools for you to use on Instagram. I highly recommend checking them out so you can get a jump start on growing your following and smashing your goals!

Free stock images

- www.pixabay.com
- www.pexels.com
- www.unsplash.com

Free Instagram story templates

- www.canva.com
- www.wordswag.co

Instagram image design guides

- https://www.huffingtonpost.ca/entry/instagram-hacks-from-people-who-take-really-good-photos_us_563a8148e4b0411d306f8393
- https://blog.iconosquare.com/create-quality-instagram-content/
- https://thepreviewapp.com/9-simple-tips-to-instantly-improve-your-instagram-feed/

9 Developing An Audience

Now that you are equipped with your chosen theme and content calendar, we need to get you set up to actively begin engaging with your audience! It is not uncommon for new users to sign up for Instagram, post amazing content, and then feel frustrated or uninspired when they find that they are not experiencing any traction on their profile. This can be extremely annoying and disheartening when you realize that you have put all of this work in and there is nothing happening! In this chapter, we are going to explore how you can connect with your target audience more effectively and develop a profile that they will be excited to interact with. While it will still take time for you to grow a massive following, these strategies will ensure that your growth is consistent and strategic.

Getting Engaged

Instagram is largely based on engagement, as this is how the algorithm determines their 'interest' signal. Although you cannot force other people to engage with your account, you can encourage it by going to their accounts and both liking and commenting on their content. By doing so, you increase the likelihood of them finding you and engaging back with your content.

A great way to take advantage of this feature in the algorithm is to spend at least 10 minutes per day engaging with people directly on your feed and then another 10 minutes engaging with new people through hashtags that are relevant to your niche. This way, you are maintaining a healthy engagement with those who you are following so that they are more likely to see you as well, thus increasing the relationships that you already have. You are also putting in the effort to interact with new accounts and make new connections by engaging on new hashtags.

While you can certainly engage in this for longer than twenty minutes per day, if you want to keep your time investment efficient, then twenty minutes is plenty. You can also use some of this time to update your story, create a new post, or watch and interact with other people's stories. The more you invest in building relationships and actively using all of the features on the platform, the more Instagram's algorithm will favor your account and increase your ability to get seen.

Using The Right Hashtags

We have already discussed how you can find hashtags, but there is another thing you need to know about when it comes to using hashtags to find your target audience. That is: you want to be using hashtags that your audience will actually be looking up, not just ones that they are using. Furthermore, you do not want to be exhaustive with your hashtags to the point that they become irrelevant. For example, if you are a food brand and you are sharing your business, tagging non-food related hashtags that are still related to your image will be a waste of your time. These will only attract people from the wrong audience and create confusion. Focus on using hashtags that are relevant to your brand and do not be afraid to branch out and use ones that may only be slightly related to the image but that are entirely related to your brand. In doing so, you increase the number of people who will see your profile and maximize your ability to connect with your targeted audience.

Diversifying Your Content

Using many different types of content and posting everywhere including your stories, feed, and IGTV is a great way to offer plenty for your audience to pay attention to. If you really want to maximize your audience engagement and grow your audience quickly, giving them plenty to look at is important. While you do not want to overwhelm your audience by uploading far too much, uploading on a consistent schedule and using all of the opportunities to connect ensures that your audience has plenty of reasons to stick around. The longer they stay on your page, the more likely they will grow interested in your brand and consider purchasing from you.

Running Ad Campaigns

Ad campaigns can be an excellent opportunity for you to connect with your target audience and grow your following quickly. If you are running a business account, using well-curated advertisements and running them consistently can help you connect with the right people quickly. Advertisements press your image out in front of new audiences quickly and help you get spotted by people who may have never seen you before, which can make them highly effective. We will talk more about how you can use paid advertisements in chapter 9.

Partnering With Other Accounts

Partnerships are a great opportunity for you to increase your visibility and get seen by a larger audience. When you collaborate with other individuals who are a part of your niche or who are sharing a similar target audience to you even if they are from a different niche, you increase your ability to get seen by your own targeted audience. You also help the person you are collaborating with get seen, too, which increases their visibility as well. This mutually beneficial marketing strategy is a great way to get found by your audience and grow quickly.

Promoting Outside Of Instagram

Just because you are focusing on Instagram does not mean that you cannot move your marketing efforts to another platform! Marketing your Instagram account on other social media platforms, on your website, or by word of mouth is a great way to help increase your followers. You can even include your Instagram handle on your business card to encourage people to locate you and follow you online. The more you talk about it and share it, the sooner you will get found by your targeted audience.

10 Advanced Promotional Techniques

Once you have begun curating a strong newsfeed and reaching out to your target audience to develop your following, it is time for you to practice promotional techniques to really get your name out there! While the practices in Chapter 8 are great for getting the word out there and building a following, they are not the only ones available to you. In fact, there are many advanced promotional techniques that you can use to begin promoting your Instagram like a pro and really experiencing a high amount of traction on your profile. In this chapter, we are going to explore what these techniques look like, how you can put them to work, and how to make sure that they are actually working for you.

Influencer Marketing Campaigns

One of the practices you can use for getting your brand out there and getting located is through using influencer marketing campaigns. Influencer marketing essentially means that you want to put your products into the hands of influencers and have *them* marketing your content, too. By having influencers sharing your products and brand with their own followers, you gain the opportunity to have your name put directly in front of their audience, too. As long as you are selecting the right influencers, their audience and your audience should be overlapping, meaning that they will help you gain access to your target audience much faster. With an influencer's seal of approval, you are far more likely to increase the effectiveness of your Instagram strategies and earn sales through your profile.

Launching an influencer marketing campaign first requires you to locate influencers who are likely to have the same target audience as you. Then, you want to consider how many followers they have and how active their following is. Influencers with more than 5,000 followers and with at least a 4% engagement rate should be considered effective early on. As you grow, you will want to continue looking for larger influencers who will be able to offer your brand even more exposure.

Influencer campaigns are costly in that you do have to offer free or discounted products to the influencers in order for them to have something to test, review, and promote to their audience. You will need to allot a budget towards this campaign that will account for the profit loss you will endure by giving away products or offering heavy discounts. However, as long as you are choosing the right influencer, this should all come back to you through their promotional activities.

Once you find influencers who appear to reflect your brand values and image and who have a similar target audience as you do, all you need to do is approach them. Typically, a well-put message that explains your intention and invites them to join your influencing opportunity is plenty enough to inspire an influencer to take you up on your opportunity. From there, you simply have to decide how much you want to give them, what you will compensate them with for their time and services, and what incentive you will provide their followers with to encourage them to purchase. The most common influencer practice for startup companies is to offer influencer deals where the influencer's products are heavily discounted and remain heavily discounted for the duration of the collaboration. Then, they are also offered a unique promo code that allows them to offer a discount to their followers, too. Lastly, many brands will also compensate their influencers 10-20% commission on all sales that come through their channel.

Paid Promotions

Paid promotions are a tool that you can use to access your following without having to put in quite so much work yourself. While a paid promotion will cost you money out of pocket, it will also take away your need to push so hard to get your paid content to perform because Instagram will automatically favor it and push it up in people's feeds due to it being paid for. Instagram's algorithm holds a certain amount of space for paid promotions across all feeds, so having the budget to invest in paid promotions actually gives you access to these exclusive paid-only spots.

As long as your paid promotion is put together effectively with an attractive image, catchy quote, and a properly chosen call-to-action button, your promotion should perform fairly well by helping you bring in more followers. You can put a paid promotion together using the Ads Manager account that can be found on your Facebook page. You will need to go to your Facebook account and locate the ads manager and then connect your Instagram account to this ads manager if you have not already. Once you have, you can go ahead and begin managing your paid promotions through this manager. The manager is highly effective in that it will walk you through the step-by-step process of building your ad, it will help you decide what you should be using or posting, and it will give you the option of cross-promoting between Facebook and Instagram if you desire. If you are going to dedicate to paid promotions, make sure you have a consistent and healthy monthly budget so that you can really get the most out of this feature. You do not want to invest your funds into paid promotions only to have them fall flat and find that you do not get as much out of it as you thought you would.

Using Your Account As A Funnel

Building your Instagram account into a part of a sales funnel is genius. In doing this, you create the opportunity for you to attract people onto your Instagram account through properly curated content and then encourage them to go over to your website in order to learn more about you and your business. If this process is built properly, your Instagram account will lead your followers to a website that will walk them through the process of learning about who you are, discovering what you have to offer, and then purchasing what you have to offer, too.

If you already have a fairly well-established online presence, adding Instagram into your sales funnel will be easy. If not, you will need to take the time to construct the rest of your funnel. The easiest way to do this is to construct a funnel that starts with your Instagram, then moves over to your website. On your website, your leads should quickly be able to determine who you are, what you value, and what you have to offer. Then, there should be a clear and easy way for them to either learn more about you or discover what you have to offer. Your website should be built in a way that walks your leads through the process of landing on your website, learning about you, and then browsing and purchasing your products. You should also have a newsletter capture on your website so that if people land on your page but do not purchase from you, they can still input their email if they want and receive updates and a reminder to come shop with you at a later time. This way, they remain in the funnel until they either choose to exit or they choose to purchase one of your products.

Split Testing Your Content

Split testing your content essentially means that you use two completely different strategies to attempt to achieve the same objective. By using two completely different approaches, complete with different captions and image styles, you are able to test to see which forms of promotion work best on your audience. Even though you may have a strong strategy in place already, it can be hard to determine exactly what your audience is going to respond to until you provide them with content so that they can physically show you by engaging with one or the other more.

You can split test your content by creating two entirely different marketing materials with the same objective and releasing them around the same time. Then, watch and see which one gets the most engagement between the two of them. For example, if you were a coffee shop you could put out one picture of a cup of coffee on a desk with some coffee beans scattered around it, complete with a funny caption. Then, you could also post an image of a coffee shop employee holding up a coffee while they smile at the camera and have it captioned with something uplifting or inspiring. You should use roughly the same hashtags for both of these images. Then, you can see which one performs the best out of the two.

By regularly using split testing you can determine exactly what your audience enjoys and gain a clearer sense on what is needed in order to draw them in and bring them to your profile. Then, all you need to do is follow the trends in those popular posts and emulate them each time in order to experience continually increasing positive results through your content!

Leveraging Your Existing Community

Using your existing community to help you build your account is a great opportunity to really get your name out there and grow your account quickly. You can leverage your followers by encouraging them to share your images by tagging their friends in them or by sharing them to their stories. You can also use giveaways or contests as a way to encourage more followers to follow you, as they will want to follow you to stay posted on your giveaway results.

Another popular thing that many brands do is create a 'movement' using a specific hashtag and an action or focus point that coincides with that hashtag. For example, Starbucks is known for their pumpkin spice lattes in the fall (*#psl*) and for having their employees write the names wrong on customers cups so that they show it on Instagram and tag it as '*#starbucksnamefail*'. Both of these are iconic and well-known across

Instagram and are entirely user-generated, despite being encouraged and promoted by Starbucks itself. That way, their community grows larger even though they themselves are not actively putting in the work to make it grow. Instead, their community is fulfilling the marketing for them through their movement.

* * *

Action Step: Building Your Advance Promotional Strategy

Now that you have a clear understanding as to how you can generate your own advanced promotional strategies on Instagram, it is time for you to actually put an official strategy together! You need to choose at least one or two different strategies out of this chapter that you are going to put to work on your profile if you are really serious about growing your account and experiencing massive traction from your efforts. If you truly want to gain the benefits of Instagram marketing, you need to go all in by employing standard practices as well as advanced ones that only highly successful businesses are using. Once you have mastered the one or two strategies, you may consider adding additional advanced promotional strategies until you are using every strategy that is relevant to your business model. That way, you really are leveraging Instagram and getting the most out of it that you possibly can.

11 Converting Your Followers

Getting followers is great, but if you are not leveraging your followers by turning them into paying customers, it is almost completely pointless. While brand recognition is important, you are in business because you have the desire to make money. For that reason, you need to value your time as an important investment and only invest it in strategies that are actually earning you serious money. In order to make Instagram worth it, you need to know exactly how you can convert your followers to paying customers and, hopefully, paying customers who want to come back to Instagram and rave about you so that you can earn even more! In this chapter, we are going to discuss how you can convert your followers to customers by building a complete sales funnel using Instagram as an essential tool for drawing in new leads.

Building The Rest Of Your Funnel

Building the rest of your funnel is going to require you to complete three additional steps after completing your Instagram account. Your Instagram account is going to be the source through which all of your new leads are going to be able to learn more about you and determine whether or not they are interested in what you have to offer. Then, if they are, they will click over to your website where they can learn even more about you and decide whether or not they want to purchase from you. So, after building your Instagram account you also need to build your website complete with an informational page, an email capture feature, and a product page, and then you will need follow-up emails.

Here is how you can add these four elements to your funnel effectively:

Informational Page

Once your lead clicks your website, you want them to immediately land on your homepage which should clarify who you are, what your brand is about, and why they should be interested in you and your products. On this page, you want to quickly and immediately convey what your image is, give a clear idea as to what your brand values are, and let them know why you are superior to any other company out there.

There are a few ways that you can achieve this on your landing page. You can either do this by offering a few highlights around these pieces of information and then offering the option to learn more, or you can do this by giving everything up front. If you choose to give everything up front, make sure that the only content you include is interesting and informative. Avoid going too deep into any back stories here or you will lose the interest of your audience.

Email Captures

Any time you set up a new website you want to have a lead capture which is going to allow your leads to leave their email address so that they can join your newsletter. This is going to ensure that if they click away from your website before purchasing anything, you have the opportunity to continue connecting with them through their inbox. That way, you can remind them about you and your products and encourage them to revisit at a later date.

Your newsletter capture should be designed so that it pops up automatically after your lead has had around 30-60 seconds to take a look at your page. By setting up this parameter, you ensure that you give your lead enough time to look at your page and decide if it is interesting to them or not. If you make the popup appear too quickly it can result in your lead feeling annoyed or bombarded and leaving your page without ever giving you their email address. If it comes up too late, they may leave the page organically before having the opportunity to leave their email address as well. Using the 30-60 second mark seems to be plenty in order to give your lead enough time to leave behind their information so that you can follow up with them later.

These days, email marketing is rampant and many people find that they are not willing to leave their email as easily anymore. The feeling of going into your inbox and having excessive newsletters building up in your account can be overwhelming and annoying, resulting in people simply not wanting to give out their email. Even if these newsletters offer value, people may be less likely to sign up for them simply because they do not want to have to sift through any more of them as they search for their other emails in their inbox. For that reason, many marketers are starting to offer incentives to encourage their leads to leave their emails. For example, a marketing strategist might offer a 3-page guide on how to grow your Instagram following, or an event planner may offer a free guide on what you need to organize in order to have a great event. By offering valuable and meaningful incentives, businesses are able to encourage their leads to actually leave behind their emails in exchange for the free incentive. As a result, you are able to gain more captures.

Product Page

After your lead has landed on your website and had the opportunity to learn more about you and give you their email, they should be offered a clear opportunity to begin searching for your products. This is typically a button or image that leads the customer away from the home page or landing page and to the page where they can browse through the products or services that are available to them.

On the product page, you want to have everything clear and attractive. You should be using high-quality product photos, clear headings that describe what the products are, and easy-to-read prices that let people know how much things cost. Your website should not be tacky, filled with animated images or texts, or covered in too many different colors or this will drive your audience away. Instead, make it look clean, simple, and easy to use.

Follow-Up Emails

The follow-up emails are essential. Ideally, you should have already designed follow up emails that are triggered to send anytime someone signs up for your newsletter so that they can be welcomed to the newsletter and offered their incentive if you were offering one. This email will sit in their inbox for a while until they check their email next, at which point it will remind them that you exist.

Next, you will also want to have an automated follow-up email that reminds people if they have abandoned their cart on your website. This simple reminder will encourage them to come back and complete the check-out process which can increase the number of sales that you complete on your page. According to a study done by Shopify, approximately 50% of abandoned carts will be retrieved through an abandoned cart email, which means that you can actually increase your sales numbers exponentially by creating this follow up.

Lastly, you should also have an automated email set to follow up with your new lead within a week of them giving you their email address. This email should simply remind them of their free incentive if you offered one and maybe give them some information about an ongoing offer you had on your website. That way, if they forgot about you then you are able to remind that lead about your brand and encourage them to come back and look again. If they were a hot lead, they will be far more likely to return this way meaning that your chances of completing a sale are exponentially increased.

Directing Your Followers To Your Funnel

Setting up your sales funnel is not necessarily enough to drive people from Instagram over to your funnel. Unfortunately, even if your sales funnel is gorgeous and insanely well crafted, simply having your email available for followers to click will not be enough to have them visit your page. While some might, not everyone is going to, so you will need to have some form of strategy for actually getting followers from your Instagram page over to your website.

A great way to increase the number of followers going to your website is to create a short and quick call to action directly in your bio. That way, anyone who lands on your page itself can quickly see what your call to action is and take advantage of it if they are interested in the offer. Saying something simple like "Grab your free eBook below!" is plenty to capture people's interest and have them clicking over to your link.

You can also increase the number of followers that convert into customers by using captions under your photo to encourage followers to go click the link in your bio. This should account for your pitch posts, where you are making actual requests for sales or action to be taken underneath your photo itself. For example, maybe once or twice a week you post a picture of one of your products and say "Check out our (product name) isn't it incredible? Check it out at our link in the bio!" If you don't want to be quite so direct, and you want to be trendy, you can also use what businesses are now using on Instagram by swapping out "Check it out at our link in the bio!" for a simple hashtag: *#linkinthebio*. This hashtag is a great way to encourage people to go check out your offer, increase your visibility, and take away the pushiness or directness out of your caption.

* * *

Action Step: Start Right Away

If you are looking to make the most out of your Instagram account and really expand your following exponentially, as well as increase your revenue through this channel, you need to start using these strategies immediately. Waiting until your following has already grown to begin building your sales funnel will result in you missing out on many excellent opportunities early on in the game. On Instagram, people who follow you are unlikely to return to your actual profile too often, which means that unless you really capture their attention through your posts you may completely miss out on several marketing activities. You want to begin generating interest right away and set the tone right from the start so that your followers know exactly what to expect on your page. That way, you are more likely to gain far more traction early on and you don't waste your time building a following of people who may forget about you before you finally present them with the opportunity to purchase from you. Even if you do not have any products available yet, you can encourage people to go to your website and learn more about you, have some form of countdown on your page, and capture leads' emails so that you can let them know when you launch. That way, you are capturing emails right away and you are drawing people into the funnel from day one.

12 Measuring Your Success

As with any marketing strategies, you always want to have a means to measure your success and determine whether or not your strategies are actually paying off. On Instagram, the way to measure your success is to use analytics. Analytics are built in to Instagram business profiles, but they are also able to be accessed through various third-party applications that can offer many additional great tools if you are interested in expanding out further. In this chapter, we are going to identify which analytics you need to care about, how you can adjust your strategy based on the analytics you identify, which third-party applications you can consider using and an actionable strategy you can use to increase your success through your metrics.

Which Metrics You Need To Care About

On Instagram, there are five metrics that you want to pay attention to when comes to tracking and monitoring the success of your marketing strategies. They are your follower growth, your audience demographics, your website clicks, your reach, and your engagement rate. Here is what they tell you:

Follower Growth
Your follower growth is simple to understand and it is a valuable piece of information for you to pay attention to. Some weeks, your growth is going

to be far greater than it will be in other weeks. Paying attention to your growth and measuring it against your recent marketing campaigns will help you determine whether they are supporting your growth or if they are falling flat in the process.

Audience Demographics

Your audience demographics are going to tell you who has been paying the most attention to your content. This can help you in two ways. First, it can help you determine who is the most likely to be interested in your unique products. Ideally, this audience should be fairly similar to the one your competitors have. Then, your audience demographics can also help you determine whether or not you are effectively reaching your target audience. If they are wildly different from who you should be targeting, you know that your strategy needs to be adjusted so that you can begin impacting the right people.

Website Clicks

Your number of website clicks is going to tell you how many people are actually interested in what you are posting enough to go to your website and learn more. This number is going to help you decide whether or not your call to actions are effective enough. If they aren't, or if your general image is not appealing to your target audience, this number is going to be incredibly low. If they are and your image is appealing and interesting, this number should be higher.

Reach

Your reach is going to help you determine how many people are actively seeing everything that you are posting on your account. Having your reach count will let you know if what you are posting is aligned enough with peoples interests that it actually captures attention and moves up in feeds. If your reach rate is low, you may be posting content that is not considered to be interesting by your targeted audience.

Engagement Rate

Your engagement rate helps you determine whether or not your content is interesting enough to actually begin earning engagement from your followers. If your reach rate and engagement rate are similar, this means that you have a high level of interest from those who are seeing your posts. If your reach rate is high but your engagement rate is extremely low, this means that you are reaching your audience but that they are not interested enough to engage with your content.

Adjusting Your Strategies As Needed

Adjusting your strategies is important as you go along with any marketing plan as it allows you to ensure that you are always getting the best reach that you possibly can. On Instagram, you will need to regularly adjust your strategy to ensure that people continue seeing your posts and that you continue rapidly growing and building connections with your followers.

The best way to determine exactly how your strategies need to be modified is to look at your existing trends based on what you have shared and the success rates you have seen and to look at your overall analytics. If you notice that your analytics suggested you performed great at one point but that you fell flat at another, you will want to go back and study what caused you to perform so well earlier on. Then, you can emulate that in your coming weeks to see if you can regain traction on your account. In the weeks that you fell flat, you should also take the time to investigate what it is that you did and why your audience may have rejected the changed approach.

As you adjust your strategy, seek to make simple adjustments and be sure to keep them small. That way, you don't accidentally overcorrect something and find yourself still struggling to regain traction. Small yet steady adjustments in the right direction will prove to be more effective as your analytics will increase, showing greater levels of engagement and interaction, proving that your strategy has been effective.

The Best Third-Party Apps For Instagram Analytics

There are many different third-party apps that you can use for tracking Instagram analytics. However, there are three that really top the charts in terms of what they offer and how they can support you in growing your following. They include PLANN, Iconosquare, and Hootsuite.

PLANN
PLANN is an application that can be used for both analytics tracking and post planning. For that reason, it can be highly valuable and effective in helping you build success in your Instagram strategy. This app will give you access to all of the same information that Instagram offers, however it does

so in an easier-to-manage-and-understand manner. Furthermore, it offers you guidance in helping you translate those metrics into action plans to help you generate greater success moving forward.

Another reason why PLANN is so effective is that you can use it to conduct research on hashtags that are relevant to your niche. PLANN offers a hashtag research bar that allows you to discover which hashtags are too popular, which hashtags are almost too popular, which ones are popular enough, and which ones are not as popular. It also allows you to curate a list of these hashtags and then copy them from the app directly into your Instagram caption which makes it extremely easy for you to complete posts faster.

Iconosquare

Iconosquare is unique in that it offers you the ability to interact with your Instagram followers directly through Iconosquare. On Iconosquare you can easily see comments that have been made on your images and you can comment directly back through the app itself. It also seamlessly connects with other social media accounts, making it easier for you to manage and promote your accounts all through one simple application.

Hootsuite

Hootsuite is another multi-account managing app that can offer great analytics when it comes to monitoring your Instagram account and its growth. Hootsuite also updates real-time, giving you access to plenty of information right away as it is happening. Furthermore, you can invite your team members onto Hootsuite so that you all have the capacity to market your Instagram account together. For larger companies, this can make Instagram account management much more effective.

* * *

Action Step: Developing Your Analytics Strategy

Now that you are aware of the importance of Instagram analytics tracking and how it can be done, you need to develop your own analytics strategy! The best way to do this is to decide how often you are going to monitor your analytics and what you are going to do in order to really monitor their growth. I suggest checking in on your analytics once per week and monitoring how your weekly posts have been going. From there, you can quickly identify what has been working and what hasn't been. That way, you can catch your Instagram before it flatlines if any of your marketing strategies are not working. Checking it any more frequently could result in you attempting to adjust something too soon, simply because it hasn't had the time to accumulate enough growth. Checking on it any less and you may find yourself overusing bad marketing strategies without having realized it because it took you too long to check in on your effectiveness.

13 Instagram Growth Hacks

The past 12 chapters have done a phenomenal job at helping you identify how you can grow your Instagram account successfully. By implementing the aforementioned tools effectively you can guarantee that your Instagram is going to blow up in no time at all. However, that doesn't mean it stops there! In this chapter, I am going to show you three additional ways that you can elevate your success on Instagram and see great results from your efforts. By implementing these additional tools you can really drive your success home and begin seeing massive and incredible results right away!

Using Automation Tools To Grow Your Account

Automation is an incredibly powerful tool that many marketers are taking advantage of because it provides them with the opportunity to quickly grow their businesses without having to put so much work into their account. By implementing automation strategies, you reduce the amount of time that you have to spend posting and engaging on your account because you allow an automated system to do it for you.

Using an app like PLANN, Iconosquare or Hootsuite allows you to plan your content in advance so that you do not have to remember to post on your account every single day at specific times. By taking your pictures in advance, you can go onto one of these third-party applications, upload your image, complete it with a caption and then generate hashtags for the post. Then, you simply schedule when you want it to be posted and your app will take care of the rest. This means that if you only want to contribute one or two days to posting the photographs you can, you do not have to feel as though you are spending every single day attempting to master the strategy and build your account.

Another way that automation can be used on Instagram is with bots. Bots can be designed to comment on other people's content when their content is similar to yours. They can also message people who follow you, thanking them for the follow and inviting them to check out your website if they feel interested in doing so. Bots can be extremely helpful in assisting you with building your Instagram page, especially if they are set up effectively. However, you do want to avoid having your automated comments or messages sound too stuffy or they will prevent you from having any success. Your comments and messages need to sound genuine and sincere so that people do not feel as though they are being spammed by a bot. That way, they are more likely to actually engage back with you and then check out your profile and your website.

Building an Instagram bot is somewhat difficult, so the best way to get one built is to have someone else do it for you. I recommend looking up experienced bot builders on websites like Fiverr or Upwork and making sure that they have plenty of positive references that prove that they are trustworthy. That way, you can employ them to create your bot for you and have it do and say whatever you desire from it. Then, all you have to do is pay them and let them get to work! In no time at all your bot will be accumulating greater attention for you and you won't even have to lift a finger to make it happen.

Building Meaningful Connections

On Instagram, your relationship with other people matters. Not only does it result in the algorithm boosting your posts up higher, but it also results in you having genuine connections that are meaningful and memorable. Remember, there are many other businesses on Instagram that are marketing to your targeted audience, too. Even though businesses only account for about 28% of Instagram's overall network, the businesses that are on there are still pretty active about going out and creating attention for themselves. You need to make sure that you are remaining competitive not by being pushy or overwhelming but by being genuine and authentic. The more meaningful and genuine your connections are with your followers, the more you are going to grow on this platform.

That being said, building meaningful relationships should not be an insincere strategy that you use to gain followers and convert leads. This should be a genuine, sincere practice that you engage in as your way to show your followers that you are grateful for them and for all that they do for you. If you show your followers love and you show them that you genuinely care for them and are appreciative of their support, they will be far more likely to continue supporting you. People respond better to gratitude and sincerity than they do to pushiness and dishonesty.

Building Through Word Of Mouth

This may seem outdated, but growing your Instagram account through word of mouth can actually be highly effective. Word of mouth has been, and always will be, one of the best ways to really get out there and get yourself in front of your audience. When you grow through word of mouth, people hear about you from those that they trust and they are more likely to genuinely care about what you have to say. This is a great way to begin your relationships off with trust without even really having to do anything to gain it.

Getting your name out there through word of mouth comes from having positive, meaningful content that people are actually interested in. Rather than simply promoting your products and services, you want to create a name for yourself so that people are more likely to remember you and talk about you. Someone is far more likely to say "Hey, do you follow (brand name)? They post so much information about this topic, I bet you would love them!" They are less likely to say "This page keeps posting these products!" Unless your products are extremely unique and speak for themselves visually, you are going to want to become known for both your products *and* your brand values. Your content is your key to achieving that.

In addition to creating valuable content that inspires people to share you with their friends, you can also promote yourself through word of mouth. Any time you are in a conversation with someone where you can organically bring it up, chat about your Instagram account and ask if they are following you yet. If not, you can let them know what your account name is and then you can go ahead and follow them back, too.

Another tool that some brands use if they have a physical business location is having an in-person sign that has their Instagram handle on it and that encourages their customers to follow them. Some also include a Following counter that shows how many fans they already have, which builds a sense of community and helps visitors feel like they want to join the following. As a result, this can build up your following quickly using a completely offline strategy.

14 Conclusion

Now that you have reached the end of this guide, I hope that you feel confident in your Instagram marketing knowledge and the strategies that are available to help you master this marketing channel. I also hope that you feel confident in the marketing strategy that you put together throughout this book, which was built in a way to help you achieve massive success with your account.

Instagram is one of the fastest growing social media platforms out there, and it offers an incredible opportunity for brands to show themselves off in a unique way. This platform is also powerful for helping you connect with your audience and build genuine relationships with them, while also expanding into the rest of your target audience at the same time. This means that not only are you building quantity but you are also building quality.

Creating a strong Instagram strategy ultimately requires you to take some time to actually research who your targeted audience is based on the nature of your business and then build from there. Building your strategy in layers, starting at the very foundation will ensure that you are building a strategy that is actually going to be strong enough to support you in achieving the growth that you desire. I hope that while reading this book you were actively following along with the action steps and completing them step-by-step. If not, I encourage you to go back and start now, beginning with chapter 1 and moving your way through this book. Building your strategy in the exact order that I have laid these steps out will ensure that you build it in a way that is foolproof. That way, you do not find that you are working with a faulty strategy and discover that you have to go back and make serious adjustments to your entire strategy to fix your mistakes.

When it comes to building your brand on Instagram, it is important that you realize that it takes time and effort. Although it can be made easier and there are ways that you can optimize your growth right from the start, getting your account to where you want it to be will take consistency and practice. On platforms like Instagram, it is rare to have overnight success, particularly because the algorithm simply is not designed to support it. Instead, your success is going to come as a result of your consistent efforts and your continued willingness to develop your strategy until you find one that works. Even then, you will need to continue adjusting your strategy as marketing trends change so that you can continually stay relevant and keep your brand growing.

Even though you are done reading this book, I want to make sure that you genuinely receive all of the benefits of having completed it. I do not want you to leave this book behind, forget about all of the great information that you have learned and then struggle to actually build a strong following on Instagram. So, I want to give you three of my best pieces of advice to help you truly master your Instagram strategy and stay strong going forward.

The first piece of advice that I want to give you is this: always focus on learning more. Take your time to learn more about marketing strategies, to learn about algorithm changes that are being made, and to learn about ways that you can optimize your work and do better. The more you stay open to learning, the easier it is going to be for you to be receptive to new strategies that are becoming available. The face of marketing constantly changes, meaning that there are always new trends and strategies that need to be followed in order for you to experience continued success. Once you get your foundation down, learning these new adjustments and practices that you can implement becomes a lot easier. So, focus on learning the basics first and then from there be willing to expand out and learn even more. The more you stay dedicated to learning and open to learning more, the more likely you are to stay on track with positive skills and experience continued growth.

The second piece of advice that I want to give you is around the art of simplicity. Although learning a new marketing strategy can be overwhelming and even challenging, I really encourage you to keep your marketing strategies as simple as possible. The more you streamline your strategies and keep them simple, the more effective they are going to be. Complex strategies are not only challenging to maintain, but they are also confusing for your audience to understand. If you attempt to do too many things at once or make it too difficult you are going to struggle to stay committed and your audience is going to have no idea what you are talking about or why they should follow you. As a result, your complex strategies are only going to result in you losing traction and not experiencing the successful results you desire. Whenever possible, make your marketing strategy as easy as it can be. Implement automation techniques, use post schedulers, keep your analytics tracking simple, and remain patient. That way, you do not sabotage your success by attempting to do too much at once.

The third and final piece of advice that I want to give you is to stay patient and committed. As you go through the process of educating yourself on marketing and checking out your competition, you might find yourself feeling envious that they are already performing so well. You may feel like you need to start producing instant results in order for you to achieve any level of success in your business. This is untrue. Not only is this unnecessary, but it is also unlikely because results simply do not happen overnight. You need to be willing to stay patient and committed and continue putting in work towards your growth consistently if you are going to experience any level of traction. Build relationships, be patient, enforce your marketing strategies, and trust that it is all working out. If you do all of this effectively, you will experience great success in building your Instagram account in no time at all. Remember, the people that you are envious about or that you are comparing yourself to online have already been marketing for a while and have had a jump start at refining their practices. It will take a bit of time for you to catch up, so be patient and give yourself and your brand the time it needs to get there. Believe that it will and put in the work to make it happen.

If you enforce these three pieces of advice and stay devoted to your Instagram account you can guarantee that you are going to experience massive success with your marketing efforts. Marketing on Instagram truly is not that hard, especially once you get the hang of it. Before you know it, you'll be amongst the influential brands that are earning incredible revenue through their Instagram account. There is no reason why you cannot be one of them unless you are unwilling to stay devoted and put in the work required. Do yourself a favor and stay committed always.

After you put this book down, I want you to go to your marketing strategy and pick just one place for you to start today. Then each day, do just one thing towards building your account. Whether you are going to devote to 20 minutes of engagement, post a new post, or create new stories, pick just one thing that you can start doing now and then move forward from there. Make sure that you actually do invest in those first two weeks of playing around with posting times and volumes so that you can get a general sense of how your account performs. Then, begin implementing your ultra-strong marketing strategy and watch your success roll in! It will happen faster than you think.

Lastly, if you enjoyed reading this book and felt that it supported you in getting a stronger understanding around Instagram and how marketing on Instagram works, I ask that you please take a moment to review it on Amazon Kindle. Your honest review of *Instagram Marketing* and the strategies that you learned in this book would be greatly appreciated.

Thank you, and I wish you the best of luck in building your Instagram account and earning massive profits through this new marketing channel that you are embracing!

Don't have time to read?

Download the audiobook for FREE today on Audible.

Then you can listen to this guide wherever you want, whenever you want.

US READERS

➡ **http://bit.ly/instagramsecretsus** ⬅

UK READERS

➡ **http://bit.ly/instagramsecretsuk** ⬅

Want to grow your personal brand?
Social Media Marketing is the key.

Discover how to dominate all social platforms in this audiobook.

Download the audiobook for FREE today on Audible.

US READERS

➡ **http://bit.ly/smmus** ⬅

UK READERS

➡ **http://bit.ly/smmuk** ⬅

Excerpt from Social Media

Marketing For Beginners 2019

Chapter 4

Understanding and Learning from Your Competitors

If you're just getting into this business, it only makes sense that there is a great advantage in identifying, understanding, and learning from your competitors. The problems you will face as a new company just now trying to get started will be problems that older, bigger companies will have already solved. Another benefit of knowing your competition is that you can use your knowledge of the industry to avoid investing time and resources into breaking into an already-saturated market. For example, if a handful of the biggest companies in the industry are aggressively competing for control of a certain audience or segment of users on social media, it's probably a good idea to avoid that market for the time being.

Keeping track of what your competitors are doing on social media can also help you refine your own brand. Compare the product or service your company is offering and compare it to the products or services of others. This can help you shape your product or service into something that is more desirable to consumers. In what aspects is your product or service better than that of your competitors? In which aspects do your competitor have a bit of an edge over you? Even if you choose not to use this information to refine or change your product or service, you can at least use it to know which aspects of your product or service you should promote and which aspects you should maybe gloss over.

Furthermore, you can carefully examine your competition's current strategies and maneuvers as well as their old ones. If you're thinking about choosing a strategy a more powerful company has already abandoned, you might want to take a close look as to why and perhaps reconsider your own strategy. Learning from other company's mistakes is playing it smart—and in this chapter, I'll offer you a simple guide on how to do it.

Identifying Your Competitors

If you're choosing to go into social media marketing to help promote your business, chances are you already have some sort of an idea of who your competitors are. But if you don't, or if perhaps you'd like to discover more of them, this section will help you identify them.

Search your own keywords and topics

Very few companies see good amounts of success in the internet age without implementing some sort of social media marketing. So there should be a good amount of companies online who offer the same type of thing you do. The easiest place to find these companies is Google. If you're selling your own scented candles, a quick good search of "scented candles" will give you a page full of results, and most of the links should take you to a competitor's website. When you're looking for competitors online, avoid large shopping platforms such as Amazon; they probably purchase their merchandise from one of your competitors anyway.

Uncover your competitors social media platforms

The next thing you should do is to research what social media platforms your competitors are most active on. This can be Facebook, Twitter, Pinterest, Instagram, or LinkedIn, just to name a few. By looking at and identifying which social media platforms your competitors are most active on, you can indirectly surmise which social media platforms will be most receptive to your own marketing strategy since you likely share the same target audience, and most companies don't like to keep posting ineffective posts on social media. If one of your competitors has a large social media following on one social media platform with a great amount of engagement and contact with their followers, this should be a sign to you that you should also have a presence on that social media platform. Once you've identified their different social media accounts across the different platforms, you can compare the posts they are making on one website with the posts they're making on others. This can help you identify the nuances between the different websites. If you keep track of, analyze, and really understand the differences between the posts on one website versus the differences on another, you can take a step back and see what works better on *this* website, and what works best on *that* website.

Understand your competitors social presence

Another thing you may want to do is to research how your competitors are viewed across social media. When you do this, you will find people with good things to say and bad things to say. If only one person says something, positive or negative, it would probably be good to ignore it. However, if you see many posts or comments saying the same thing, it might be something you might want to take into account. By doing this, you can identify which strategies from which companies are working to generate a positive view of themselves among their target audience. At the same time, you can also see the things companies can do, on or off social media, to generate a negative view of them among their target audience.

Make a list of your competitors

Once you've identified as many competitors as you can find, write their names down on a piece of paper, a word document, or an excel sheet. For the next step, you will again need a Social Media Analytics tool. Again, Spredfast works well for this as they offer different tools for different social media platforms. If you want some statistics on one of your competitors Facebook pages, Spredfast's Facebook Competitor Report will give you all the information you need, from the number of messages your competitors Facebook page sends out and the types of posts they make to influences, rates of engagement, followers gained or lost, and mentions. Spredfast also has the Twitter Comparison Report to find all these same statistics on Twitter as well as the Instagram Competitors Report that gives you all these same statistics on Instagram.

Gather relevant analytics about your competitors performance

Once you have this information on hand, write down the different statistics in columns by the name of the company. This will make it easy for you to discern what companies have the most effective strategies. A good way to measure this is to see how many times a post was engaged with and divide that by the number of times the post was seen. Say a post was viewed 10,000 times and clicked on 3,000 times. Take the 3,000 times it was clicked on or 'engaged with' and divide it by the 10,000 times it was seen and you get .3, which, of course, means that 30% of impressions ended in clicks. Repeat this process for as many different posts on as many different accounts as you can. The highest percentages are the most effective posts.

How to Use Your Competitors' Information

Now that you have a clear idea of which posts by which companies ended in the highest percentages of engagements per impressions, you can focus on the 10 or 15 posts which had the percentages. Having all these different types of information will greatly improve not only your knowledge of the industry but will also offer opportunities to refine your strategy based on what other companies have done right and what they have done wrong. Hopefully, there will be specific aspects of certain businesses strategies and marketing campaigns that stand out as exceptionally effective and successful. Predicting that the market will be responsive to these strategies based on past events, you can spend your resources on plans that have a much greater chance of succeeding than others.

One thing you should also consider on social media is how your competitors are representing themselves on these platforms. Look at their descriptions of themselves. How are they approaching their social media presence? What is the tone of their posts? Looking at how your competitors represent themselves, as well as how successful their presence on social media platforms is, should give you an idea as to how receptive your target audience is to various tones and representations. Look at how they've customized their page. What is their aesthetic? What kind of images are they including in their posts on social media? Are they humorous? Or are they more serious and sentimental?

Look at the different types of descriptions they're using to describe their company, product, or service. You should also look at their social media presence as they change their brand. Companies spend a lot of time, effort, and money in rebranding, and looking at how your competitors have chosen to rebrand themselves can give you an idea of the state of the market. Another thing you should look for is how they promote new products or services over social media. You should analyze the angle of their approach and try to develop an understanding of what needs they're trying to meet by marketing on these social media platforms.

You should also look at how they act and behave on social media. How do they engage with other users on social media? You can analyze how they deal with negative comments and use that information to shape your own social media marketing strategy. Look at how they act on social media. Do they respond to people making jokes? Or do they try to present themselves as more serious than that? You can identify the different ways they prompt their followers on social media to engage with them. Once you have a good understanding of how much and in what way your competitors engage with their audience, you should now take in to consideration how large their following is across social media websites. Compare your competitors against each other. Who has more followers? Which strategy seems to be working? Is that a strategy you think may work for your business?

All of these posts may take a different angle on advertising, and they may all have different messages and use different means of perking interest. Analyze them one at a time, and compare the post to the other ones made by the same company. What is different about this ad? What does it have that the other posts do not? What doesn't it have that the other posts do have?

Besides analyzing your competitor's advertisements, you should also look at their special offers. Using social media analytic tools, you can identify which special offers were popular and which ones weren't as popular. In addition to giving you ideas for special offers you can give out to your own customers, it can also give you a very good, indirect insight into what your customers value in your product and service. It can also show you what things will actually get them to act and purchase something or sign up. You can use tools such as SEMrush (https://www.semrush.com/) to gather insights about your competitors. Practical Ecommerce has written an article about how you can view all of your competitors ads on Twitter and Facebook. (https://www.practicalecommerce.com/see-competitors-ads-facebook-twitter)

Analyzing and attempting to reverse engineer the strategies behind these posts is a very worthwhile endeavor. Because you are selling the same kind of product, you likely have a similar target audience, and these hyper-successful ads are hard evidence of what works. This isn't to say that you should simply copy their post. You should never plagiarize. Having that reputation in the company can easily be disastrous. The key is to isolate the aspects of the post that are missing from the other posts on their social media account.

For example, if it's a humorous post, and that same humor is not found in other posts on their account, try to discern exactly what kind of humor it is. Is the humor dark? Slapstick? Self-deprecating? Understanding what kind of humor they used at the same time provides you with information as to what kind of humor your target audience is receptive to. Remember, if you chose to derive inspiration from another company's social media posts, you should always make sure to be completely original in delivery. It's fine to make a post in the same vein as another company's post; it is not fine to take someone else's idea without permission.

If you isolate what made the post or advertisement so successful, and you do this for 15 different, successful social media posts, you have a good jumping off point to develop your own ads and strategy. This is not to say that success is ensured; all it means is that your target audience has been receptive to posts or ads with these certain attributes in the past. There's no promise that they will necessarily be receptive to your post or ad. Probably one of the most important parts of this whole process is making sure you understand exactly what made that post so much more successful than the ones before or after it. It may be that it has many things he other posts before or after it; so you really have to dig in and analyze what made it stand out. To do this, read the comments, see what people are saying about it. If they shared it, why did they share it? If they retweeted it, why did they retweet it? Remember that the single most important aspect of this process is developing an understanding of your target audience. If you're able to gain a deep understanding of what they like and what they're receptive to, it makes your strategy much more informed and, therefore, effective.